$15.98
MW00700591

previous page: Denise Dixon, negative strip

Wendy Ewald
Secret Games

Collaborative Works with Children 1969–1999

Preface by Adam D. Weinberg and Urs Stahel

Scalo Zurich – Berlin – New York
in association with
Addison Gallery of American Art
Center for Documentary Studies at Duke University
Fotomuseum Winterthur

This publication is supported in part by funds provided by the Lyndhurst Foundation to the Center for Documentary Studies at Duke University.

The exhibition, *Wendy Ewald: Secret Games, Collaborations with Children, 1969–1999,* has been funded in part by generous grants from the National Endowment for the Arts, a federal agency, SAM Sustainability Group (www.sam-group.com) and Volkart Foundation. Additional funding has been provided by John Ryan III, Warren Coville, MIGROS Cultural Percentage, Swisscom AG, Bern, Foundation Zurich Insurance Group and Bickel Reklamen.

Exhibition Venues:

April – June, 2000
Fotomuseum Winterthur, Winterthur, Switzerland

April – June, 2001
Museet for Fotokunst, Odense, Denmark

September – December, 2001
Addison Gallery of American Art, Andover, Massachusetts

January – March, 2002
The Corcoran Gallery of Art, Washington, D.C.

June – August, 2002
Museum of Art, Rhode Island School of Design, Providence, Rhode Island

September – December, 2002
Kemper Museum of Contemporary Art, Kansas City, Missouri

Luis Arturo González, negative strip (top); Diamel Vargas, negative strip (bottom)

If Complications Arise . . .

The history of photography exhibits a conspicuous tradition of tension between photographer and subject. Documentary photographers have always been especially concerned with minimizing the distance and maximizing the intimacy between themselves and their material in order to make the most honest, unmediated portraits possible — encouraging, in effect, their subjects to speak for themselves.

This uneasy dialectic of pictorial interrogation and response dates from photography's earliest days. The state of nineteenth-century photographic art did not promote spontaneity or agility. Cameras were cumbersome; emulsion was so slow that it took a paralyzingly long time to obtain a properly exposed plate. Still, it must be said that the greatest divisions between photographer and subject were cultural. Differences in race, ethnicity and class created a formidable gap, much as they do today.

This dissonance derived from the power — explicit and implicit — that photographers immediately came to exert over their subjects. As photography entered the realm of the ordinary, a working credo took shape based on largely unchallenged cultural assumptions and the mystique of the aimed machine. The new photographic belief system was not very different, really, from earlier fine-arts ethics/esthetics. It went something like this: The photographer controls the image of the person being photographed through pose, angle, exposure, etc. Even a candid photograph is structured, no matter how loosely. The subject is affected by the presence of the photographer and by the very fact of being observed. Wittingly or unwittingly, subjects relinquish their power over pictures of themselves. How they are seen, who they are seen by, and in what context they are seen — all these crucial determinants are decided by the photographer.

Very early on, certain photographers attempted to alter this imbalance. They realized that the more familiar they were with their subjects, the better chance they had of seeing inside their lives. In an attempt to establish more authentic connections with people they wanted to photograph, some photographers lived for extended periods near or with their subjects — a style of working that bears some resemblance, in process and result, to the Method Acting of the American stage.

In 1936 Walker Evans started making photographs for what was to become *Let Us Now Praise Famous Men.* On assignment for *Fortune* magazine, he and the writer James Agee took up residence with three tenant farmer families in Alabama. Both men knew that their motives were suspect. They acknowledged the ambiguities of their relationship with the families; indeed, they developed an almost agonizingly acute sensitivity to the ways in which their subjectivity affected their reporting. In what might be characterized as repeated paroxysms of conscience, Evans and Agee kept reminding themselves that they were not in any essential way distinct from or better than their subjects — except for the crucial difference that they were outsiders. "If complications arise," Agee cautioned, "that is because the authors are trying to deal with their subject not as journalists, politicians, entertainers, humanitarians, or priests, or artists, but seriously."

Let Us Now Praise Famous Men changed photography once and for all. Whatever effect the authors' candor might have had on their subjects, the pretense of journalistic objectivity was dropped entirely. From then on it would be increasingly difficult for photographers to assume authority over their subjects. Henceforth, their privileged position would be in question — if not summarily judged to be downright exploitative.

It is not surprising that Wendy Ewald, who admired Evans and Agee when she was a student, chose the Appalachian South as the site of her first extended project. In 1975, in Kentucky, she founded the Mountain Photography Workshop and began working with children between the ages of six and fourteen. Ewald spent six years in Appalachia; it was here that she established the roots of her practice. She wrote that when she arrived she wanted "to make a document of my new community, but the camera seemed to get in the way." Her instincts, along with her experience of working on Canadian Indian reservations, led her to believe that she might better manage her project by removing herself as the exclusive author and providing her students with tools and skills to document their own lives.

Other photographers were teaching children to take, develop, and print their own pictures, but few regarded this work as more than a pedagogical exercise in skill development and creative expression. Ewald came to understand that she wanted to do more than provide students with an outlet; she wanted to challenge fundamental, categorical distinctions between art and documentary photography, between photographer and subject, child and adult. Her extended commitment amounted to a continuing collaborative exploration. Artistically, the important difference in her approach stemmed from the realization that by handing over "the means of production" she could erase a good deal of the distance between artist and subject. Additionally, and paradoxically, she stepped away from the old polarities of subject-object-author. In doing this, she did not get closer in some formulaic sense; she simply left the stage — the photographic set — to the children.

In 1985 Ewald produced *Portraits and Dreams*, a collection of images and writings by the children of Whitesburg, Kentucky. The book made it clear that like Evans and Agee before her, Ewald was dealing with her subject "seriously". (And, as in the case of Evans' and Agee's book, *Portraits and Dreams* took a long time to find a publisher. When at last it did, reviewers began calling it "an American classic.")

Though Ewald would admit to being socially committed, she has reservations about the power of photographs to effect political change. Accordingly, she has encouraged her collaborators to explore their dreams and fantasies as well as the day-to-dayness of their sometimes troubled existence. Solo photography and collaborative work aside, her role as author has often been as editor — selecting images and writings for exhibition and publication which are then orchestrated into a larger work, which is neither polemical nor political. Ewald provides the impetus, the framework, the vehicle for the students' ideas, expressions, and images. Her eloquently unadorned introductions to each of her books forthrightly reveal the situations, terms and structure out of which the book arises. Nothing is concealed from the reader, neither motive nor method.

Framing her process in this way, Ewald reinforces the impression that her collaborative work, while complicated, preserves and enhances the visions she has elicited from her collaborators. In this respect it is quite different, obviously, from the kitsch photography of adorable children that characterizes humanitarian projects, the sort of product that confirms packaged ideas about innocence.

Innocence is such an awesomely complicated condition that we tend to welcome assurances that children are, at the very least, developmentally predictable, that at any given time there are certain essential experiences they cannot know. The sometimes menacing images produced by Ewald and her students do not bolster this assurance. And there is in her vision a consistently uncanny directness that sets it apart from the work of other photographers (Lewis Hine, Helen Levitt and Sally Mann come to mind) who deploy images of children directed at grown-up sensibilities that are not always accessible to their young subjects. Ewald's children are, if you will, in on the joke — even when, as is so often the case in her books and exhibitions, the joke is rather grim.

Ewald's working approach has been evolutionary. Initially she felt it necessary to remove herself from the photographer-subject equation. She exhibited her images separately from those of the students; her photographs were appended to rather than integrated with their work. But she sensed something was missing by not acknowledging and including her own voice.

It would seem that she found a balance between her own work and the work of her students while doing projects abroad, many of them involving women. The variety of her collaborative projects — since Kentucky, Ewald has worked in many parts of the US as well as in Latin America, Europe, Asia and Africa — upsets the assumption that children — or women, for that matter — can be expected to say essentially the same things wherever they are. The visions of the Dutch children Ewald worked with, for example, are as different from the visions of, say, her Indian students as the portraiture of Julia Margaret Cameron is from the crypto-scientific studies of Eadward Muybridge.

By the time her third book, *Magic Eyes*, was published in 1992, Ewald's photographs were mingled with those of the Colombian children she was teaching. The images were interspersed with a biographical text narrated by a woman Ewald had come to know. In *Magic Eyes*, as in the present book, one is often confused as to whether a particular photograph is made by Ewald or by a collaborator (captions and photo credits appear at the back of the book). The result is an intricate admixture of visions that weave in and out of the text in almost hallucinatory fashion.

The unsettling variety of Ewald's work with so many different people is in line with the ethnology developed by Lévi-Strauss, Bateson, Mead, and others. Even in Kentucky, she "gets pictures" inaccessible to the customary techniques of Western reportage. Of course, she is not doing reportage at all, but a delicate kind of collaborative dreaming, in which the resultant images seem to draw their force directly from underlying cultural tensions. Esthetically, the pictures are of astonishingly high quality. Unencumbered by conventions of good picture-taking, Ewald's imagery displays a freshness and abundance of imagination that calls into question the value (not to mention the values) of high-polish image making. To categorize this as children's art would be to shortchange the depth and subtleties of its effects. Nor would it do to cite Joseph Beuys' coy remark to the effect that everyone is an artist. Perhaps one should simply say that there is a robust mystery afoot in the force of Ewald's work, as there is in all successful art, and that what we are confronting here is a dramatic, vital development in the disassembly of the Olympian artist.

When Ewald's images are placed on equal footing with those of her students, we experience her voice as one among many. We are required to guess who is the photographer. This approach keeps the question of authorship in the foreground. It destabilizes the viewer's expectations. We cannot take for granted who is seeing and who is being seen. It is also not clear who is the teacher and who is the student. A concept may begin with Ewald, but how it is developed depends in large measure on the students themselves. The relationship between photographer and student is reciprocal rather than hierarchical.

This is one of the ways in which Ewald's ongoing project is as much conceptual as documentary. Documentary photography, as the term itself implies, emphasizes the photographic object as evidence, as accurate accounting. One could readily situate Ewald in the stream of documentary photography that includes Walker Evans, Robert Frank, Larry Clark, and Nan Goldin. But there is a surprising element in her work that draws on the currents of conceptual art. As in images by conceptualists such as Bruce Nauman, Douglas Huebler and Sol LeWitt, Ewald's projects emphasize "the idea" and "the process" rather than the singular object. Here, the photograph is an instrument of the idea.

The conceptual nature of Ewald's work also connects her to artists of her own generation. Imagery of childhood has been used by Tracey Moffatt, Gillian Wearing, Nic Nicosia, Robert Gober, Martin Honert and Mike Kelley to undermine categorical notions about the child, and to reconsider the traumas and fantasies of youth.

Ewald herself cites Mike Kelley as a point of reference. Her work derives from
the tradition of documentary photography, Kelley's from performance art and music. But
their goals converge in the attempt to draw attention to what is usually considered
beneath attention. Kelley's diverse, anarchic productions often rely on the handmade and
the homemade, and this — wedded to a conceptual approach — forces the viewer to
reassess realms of artmaking that have been relegated to the sidelines, to re-examine
the stuff of childhood memories and the differences between high art and craft. Kelley's
non-idealistic art is about loss and transgression, and with him, ultimately, the anonymous remains anonymous. Ewald's work, on the other hand, feels more affirmative,
giving individual voice to the anonymous.

The artist who most bears comparison to Ewald is Gillian Wearing. Although
somewhat younger than Ewald, Wearing too has built her vision by playing against
the pseudo-objectivity of documentary photography and film. She sets out to make
her subjects complicit in the image-making, and has invented a number of conceptual
projects that combine her voice with those of her subjects. And with Wearing, as with
Ewald, each work is a self-contained unit, yet each stems from preceding ones.

It is instructive to compare Ewald's video *Memories from the Past Centuries* (1999)
with Wearing's *10-16* (1997), in which Wearing lip-synchs the voices of children to
videos of adults. Wearing's video reflects the development of children from pre-
adolescence to adolescence. Particularly as it pertains to attitudes about sex, violence,
friends, and family, Ewald's video starts from a different premise. She gave youngsters
from North Carolina photographs and case histories of Jewish children who had
survived the Holocaust. She asked them to write brief narratives in the voices of
Jewish children, of Nazi sympathizers, and as witnesses. The students then addressed the
video camera as these personae.

While both Ewald and Wearing start from fact — Wearing from the narratives
of the children and Ewald from the case histories — the approach and results are quite
different. In Wearing's project we are in doubt as to who is doing the talking — Wearing,
the child or the adult. By literally putting voices in people's mouths, Wearing causes
the viewer to consider the child within the adult. In Ewald's dual-screen installation,
we see a photograph of the Holocaust survivor on one screen and a present-day child
role-playing on the other screen. While we are not confused as to who is saying what,

there is an unsettling slippage between the children's perception vis-à-vis the reality of the historical figure they are portraying. Ewald's project is about history, cultural stereotypes, misperceptions and power, while Wearing's work is more personal and psychological. Ewald's minimally manipulative relationship with her subjects ensures we do not lose sight (literally and metaphorically) of her collaborators, their individuality, ideas and feelings.

The old definition of documentary photography as an objective, personally uninflected statement is moribund. Documentary today — as an image of a subject negotiated by the maker — is flourishing. Artists like Ewald have held onto the notion that documentary truths can be conveyed. Those truths, however, are not separate nor easily distinguishable from her own vision and perceptions. "Sometimes I think I disguise myself as a teacher," Ewald has written, "in order to make the pictures I need to see." Perhaps this is Ewald's secret game — to perceive the world through others' perceptions as much as her own, to make her work their work, and their work her own.

ADAM D. WEINBERG
The Mary Stripp and R. Crosby Kemper Director,
Addison Gallery of American Art

URS STAHEL
Director of Fotomuseum Winterthur

Denise Dixon, negative strip

The library wall

Introduction

The walls of the library in the house where I grew up in Michigan are covered with photographs documenting the lives of my mother and father and their six children. The earliest pictures of me were taken by photographers employed by the General Motors Corporation, whose very first ad campaigns my grandfather's agency had produced. In the early decades of the automotive industry, my grandfather had figured out that images were more effective than words in selling products, and on this then-revolutionary notion he built an enormously successful career in advertising.

In addition to the family pictures on our library walls there are many black-and-white photographs shot for the society pages of the local newspaper: my parents' wedding, a family vacation to Arizona, and our favorite — a picture of my parents feeding a pig in a swank Parisian restaurant.

Examined chronologically, the pictures become less formal with the years, and in later years there are more color snapshots taken by family members, not so many by professionals.

My first camera was a Brownie given to me by my grandmother Harriet when I was eleven. Earlier that year, during the Cuban missile crisis, one of my younger brothers was hit by a car while coming home from school. He suffered some neurological damage. In the course of playing with him in the hospital, I devised a wheelchair game of stop-and-go using my handmade drawings of a stop light. It was the first step in helping him regain his speech, and it was then that I began to understand the teaching power of visual symbols.

A year later, my father, who had always been interested in sports, began managing prize fighters, and my family started frequenting boxing arenas. (My mother, father and I were usually among the few white people in the crowd.) In the second round of the first fight I saw, my father's fighter, a heavyweight named Sonny Banks, knocked down his promising opponent, Cassius Clay. The fighters and trainers in my father's circle became family friends; many of them spent Christmas Eve at our house, singing carols around my pink piano. Ringside photographs began to appear on our library walls.

Two years after my brother was hurt, a second family tragedy occurred: Sonny Banks was killed in the ring. He took a hard uppercut, his head hit the canvas at an odd angle, and his brain stem was fatally damaged. Sonny was twenty-four. My mother never went to another fight. Though my father quit managing for a while, he couldn't stay away from the ring for long. As a teenager, I became his companion at the fights, at press conferences, and social events centered on boxing.

When my father died a few years ago, I discovered that he had kept every photograph and newspaper story from those years, next to souvenirs of his children's early years. Among his memorabilia of the boxing years was Sonny Banks' unused plane ticket from Philadelphia, where he died, back home to Detroit.

I began making photographs seriously when I was seventeen, photographing my brothers and sisters with a tripod-mounted 4 x 5 Crown Graphic purchased from a classmate. I had seen the pictures she had made with it and I was excited by their sharper-than-reality quality. I knew I wanted to be an artist and I was thrilled when I understood that I could use the medium that I was most familiar with to tell my own family story. When it became time for me to go to college, I decided to study art at a school that required students to work in the world as well as study in the classroom. After some time I enrolled in an education course, thinking I might need to teach in the future. (I skipped so many classes in order to work in the darkroom that I almost flunked.)

When I completed my studies and first began to work as an artist, it was natural for me to think about the connections between myself and the people I was making pictures of, and reflect on ways the photographic encounter affected both of us. I wanted to make photographs that were immediate and revealing — different from traditional portraiture that called for formal distance between artist and subject.

Since that time when I first began photographing, I have heard many times, in many languages, children and adults say, "I want to take a picture" — when what they meant was, "I want to be photographed." Who or what is it, I asked myself, that really makes a photograph — the subject or the photographer?

Working with my injured younger brother was the start of my lifelong interest in children. My work as a photographer using pictures to teach them began in 1969, when I was offered a job working with children on an Indian reservation in Canada. I remembered the excitement I experienced as a child with my Brownie camera. I traveled to the reservation, wanting to see what kinds of pictures the Naskapi children would take.

When I saw their first pictures, I knew they had a raw power that I had yet to see in photographs. Their work led me to wonder if I could consciously merge the subject of a picture and the photographer, and create a new picture-making process.

From St. Augustine to Wordsworth to contemporary psychologists, thinkers have pondered the complex and seemingly uninhibited world of childhood. To ask the children themselves to participate in my exploration of their world, I thought, would be to acknowledge that it is *their* experience, and that rather than being made to "mind their place," children might be helped to find ways of illuminating and sharing their inner lives.

I embarked on a series of teaching sojourns to various parts of the world which would take up the next thirty years of my life. I knew, of course, that there were risks in guiding children toward genuine artistic expression. There was the risk of challenging a hierarchical and exclusively adult vision of our common humanity. There was the risk of buttoning up in the abstract all uncertainties about innocence, art, and personal integrity.

Yet the children quickly taught me that art is not a realm where only the trained and formally accredited may dwell. The truly unsettling thing about the children's imagery was that, despite their inexperience with what adults might call rational thinking, their images tapped into certain universal feelings with undeniable force and subtlety. The inventiveness of their work held my fascination and began to direct my own picture-making.

How different were the two kinds of photography, theirs and mine? Clearly, there was a radical difference between interrogation-by-the-camera and response-by-the-subject. This led me to believe that in working with others I had to learn to recognize what they were seeing, and what kind of questions their vision asked of the world. These questions kept me going. It was like learning a new language, and it took a great deal of patience. Each child and each culture seemed to have a different sense of composition — determined, it often seemed, by the landscape and the interiors of their homes. Many times I despaired seeing what was going on until one image, a portrait of two grandmothers shaking hands in South Africa, for instance, unlocked the visual language I was living in the midst of. Then I could begin to understand and create a context for the images. Gradually I saw that it was less interesting for me, as an artist, to frame the world wholly according to my own perceptions. I wanted instead to create situations in which I allowed others' perceptions to surface with my own.

My two grandmothers, they was happy. — Franklin Monnakqtla

Canada 1969 – 1974

During the summer of 1967, there were riots in Detroit. One of the fighters my father managed was arrested for looting and released in my father's custody. The riots changed Detroit and made me aware of its racial divide. The next summer, I volunteered to work in a settlement house in the city.

I was assigned to work with a team teaching black history in a program designed to keep high-school students who had gotten into trouble off the streets. I was barely as old as my students. I gave myself the task of creating a visual documentation of African history. As a result, I was privileged to find myself surrounded by the Black Power movement.

When I graduated from high school the following spring, I was eager to know more of the world, and still interested in issues of race. I got a job working with children on a Native American reservation in Canada. The Polaroid Foundation had just begun giving out cameras and film to teachers of what used to be called "underprivileged" children.

It was 1969, three years before the American Indian Movement took hostages at Wounded Knee and demanded investigations into the treatment of native people. Americans knew very little about Native American people and their ways of life. My image of American Indians came from the few photographic anthologies in print at that time, the ones displaying romantic images of chiefs, braves, and adorable children. What I saw in Canada was different. I saw my contemporaries caught between two cultures, with no jobs, inadequate housing, dwindling supplies of game, and pandemic alcoholism. That summer I grew preoccupied with ways of showing what reservation life was like while, at the same time, respecting my students' privacy and their ways of looking at their own lives.

I set up an afternoon photography class for the children. Each child took a camera and a pack of film. About fifteen of us walked around the reservation. I took pictures of the children and their families, working selectively and cautiously. The children, on the other hand, took pictures of everything they saw: the chief, drunk, trying to saw a board; a young couple fighting; a tea pot on a windowsill; a great-aunt in her white Sunday dress sitting on the rocks by the shore. The children's pictures were more complicated and disturbing than mine, and closer, I realized, to what their life was like.

One afternoon, a fourteen-year-old boy named Merton Ward and I decided to photograph the cemetery. Merton divided his time between the reservation and South Boston, where his mother lived. He told me he had been deported from the US for busting parking meters, so now, when he crossed the border, he had to use a false name. He knew more about the outside world than others on the reservation. Perhaps because I was from that world, we became close friends.

Merton took his Polaroid Sharp Shooter, I had my Crown Graphic. We began casually photographing the whole graveyard, then moved in closer to take pictures of Merton's grandmother's grave. I centered the white tombstone and shot it slightly from above, so that the stone was framed by grass. In the background, on either side of the stone, you could see a white cross.

Merton squatted down and took his picture from below, placing the headstone far to the right, so that it veered out of the frame. His tombstone looms over the viewer, looking as if it is about to take off.

My image shows what a Native American graveyard looks like. You can read the inscription on the gravestone and see the simple handmade crosses in the background. Merton's picture doesn't do that. It is grainy, washed-out, and the proportions are "wrong." But his cemetery is a frightening place. No one goes there — or if they do, they often see ghosts.

That afternoon in the cemetery was a turning point. Although Merton did not consciously compose his photographs to reflect his feelings, I realized his pictures portrayed reservation life more accurately and expressively than mine.

While I was coming to an important personal discovery, the world around me was changing, and the racial situation between whites and

Native Americans grew tense. I sensed that the presence of my camera made my friends uncomfortable. Merton and the other children didn't hesitate to photograph the often painful situations they were living through, but I rarely photographed on the reservation after that day in the graveyard. Instead, I spent the summers of my college years teaching photography to Native American children, collecting their pictures, and tape-recording stories told to me by the adults on the reservation.

When I think now about the photographs Merton and I made, mine reminds me of the magic I associated with that neat little graveyard. Merton's makes me think of the young men I knew who died violent alcoholic deaths during the summers I worked on the reservation, and how Merton had to guide me to one of the coffins, and how frightened I was to look into the young man's face.

Proposal for Polaroid Project
New Brunswick, Canada
Summer 1973

I propose to run a photography class for Indian children ages four to sixteen. The program will involve fifty children for six weeks. I will work with groups of five to six children at a time. The intention is for the children to document with photographs and words their feelings about their lives. To carry this out, I feel I need eight cameras and 150 to 200 film packs.

The object of this proposal is the reservation of Black River, New Brunswick. There are approximately 800 people on the reservation; a good percentage are under sixteen years of age. The reservation is located between two very small towns, one French and the other English. Because of racial tension, there is no interaction with these towns, which severely limits recreation for both adults and children. On the reservation itself there are no organized activities or facilities for recreation. As there is little to occupy the children, many of them make up games like baseball using sticks and stones. But unfortunately most children, unless forced inside by their parents, spend their nights roving the reservation in gangs, taunting the police, smashing bottles, drinking, and smoking. During the day, they sleep.

The children attend school on the reservation until the seventh grade. After that, they may attend a white school sixty miles away. At this point, most of them stop their education. They become embarrassed and discouraged in a foreign environment. They receive appalling treatment from many students and teachers in the white school; yet the prospect of life on the reservation with no education is just as frightening.

Many of the girls are pregnant when they leave school. As there is no birth control, this is the beginning for them of a ten-to-twelve child family. All hopes for more educa-tion or a better type of life are forgotten. The boys may be lucky enough to get a job for a couple of months logging on Indian land, but more likely they will watch television during the day or sleep, and drink at night.

Most people receive welfare. I lived with a family of five on welfare. They were rarely able to buy meat or vegetables, even though they used their money wisely and never drank. The Indians must buy their houses from the federal government. New houses are

slowly being built. Most people, however, live in old dilapidated wooden houses with
no plumbing. The houses have two to three bedrooms which accommodate approximately
twelve people. I have been to some houses with no furniture except for a bed, because
each time the alcoholic mother or father needed a drink they traded a piece of furniture
for a bottle of wine. In some places there is urine and excrement on the floors because
the parents have left small children unattended for days while they drink. These living
conditions cause outbreaks of tuberculosis and hepatitis. Generally, the people of Black
River fear doctors and hospitals. They associate hospitals with death, so medical attention
is rare, and disease spreads easily.

I have lived on the reservation for two summers, and have also spent two months
on another reservation in Labrador. During this time I have collected pictures and
writings done by the children. I and others who have seen this collection feel it is pro-
found and enlightening, and should be made available for many people to see. My
intention this summer is to finish this project by collecting more photographs, writings,
and taped interviews, and to gather them into book form with the children's help.

I feel strongly that the people of Black River should be able to make a book
for white people and for other Indians, a book explaining how they live. At this point
in Indian-white relations, it is necessary for white people to understand the Native
American way of life, not from an outsider's viewpoint, but directly from the people
themselves. I have looked at many photographs of Native Americans, but I have never
seen the depth present in the pictures taken by the children of Black River. A photog-
rapher or anthropologist may come to an Indian community for months or a year,
but he will not spend his whole life living on a reservation. A feeling of endurance and
joy in spite of hardship is what makes the children's photographs more true, more
revealing than the transient professional's. If we, as non-Indians, are going to try
to deal with situations like Wounded Knee and also our own personal prejudices,
it is necessary to have direct, honest information about the situation and feelings of
Native Americans.

Wendy Ewald
Yellow Springs, Ohio

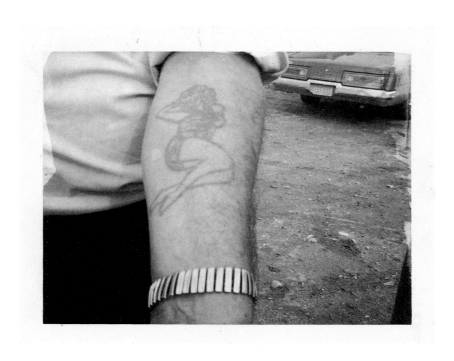

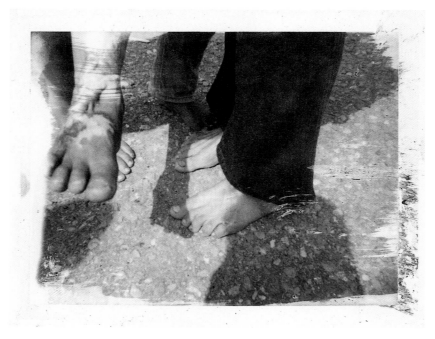

Photographs by Terry Augustine, Annabelle Joe, Deborah Joe,
Benedict Michelle, Larry Mitchell,
Stafford Paul, Esther Ward, and Merton Ward

Kentucky 1975–1982

In the early 1970s, along with many other young people, I migrated to San Francisco right after leaving college. But I soon became disillusioned with the rootlessness of what seemed like paradise to everyone around me. One evening I saw some documentary films made by a group of Appalachian filmmakers about their neighbors and friends. I was particularly struck by a short film about hog killing; its roughness and immediacy reminded me of the Canadian children's photographs.

A few months later, with trepidation, I moved to Kentucky to work with the collective of filmmakers, artists and musicians who had made these striking films. I rented a small house on Ingram's Creek, one of the most beautiful and remote hollers in Kentucky's Letcher County.

Aside from the four or five families that had settled the area a century ago, no one else had ever lived on Ingram's Creek. Bit by bit, however, the neighbors welcomed me. I grew close to many of the women I met. I tried to emulate their stoicism and spirituality as an alternative to the values of the tanned, slim country-club women I had grown up with.

My old sense-memory of summer—the hum and gurgle of air conditioning—was replaced by the sounds of crickets and screen doors slapping shut. I grew my hair long like some of the older women—Bertha, Callie, Rena, and Luveena—in ringlets down to my waist. They didn't cut their hair because the Bible told them it was sinful. Yet there was an easy sensuality among the women. They took me on as their daughter and taught me what it was for them to be women: they taught me to protect myself and obey God. Their own daughters, on the other hand, wanted a piece of the suburban culture I had left behind.

I continued teaching photography to children, this time in three elementary schools, Kingdom Come, Campbells Branch and Cowan. Kingdom

Rena's grandchildren

Come was one of the last one-room schools in Kentucky. It had survived consolidation because the buses couldn't bring children down the rough road out of the holler to a larger school. The students at Kingdom Come studied in small groups: Freddy Childers and Billy Dean Ison in the first grade, Shirley Couch in the second grade, Amy Cornett, Mary Jo Cornett and Tammy Williams in the third and fourth grades. The older children helped the younger ones.

Before starting to teach the fourth-grade class at Campbells Branch, I was warned by the regular teacher that these children had the lowest IQs in the entire school. They turned out to be the most talented group I have ever worked with.

In my classes I wanted to create a lively, open atmosphere so that the students would feel at home expressing themselves. I knew that the children, like artists, were more inspired at certain times than at others. They needed to have their cameras always with them, along with plenty of film, so that when they wanted to photograph something—a hog killing, the birth of a colt, or a birthday party—they could do it. For the most talented of them, picture-taking could become part of their lives, and especially of their play.

We built darkrooms at the two larger schools—Campbells Branch and Cowan. At Cowan, the only space available was the boiler room. When the coal-fired furnace kicked in, I had to yell to be heard over the roar. We hooked hoses up to the water tanks and ran them along the floor so we could mix chemicals and wash negatives. When the hoses sprung leaks, coal dust mixed with the water and covered the floor with gray sludge. We had four new enlargers and a stabilizer that developed, fixed, and spit out dry prints in ten seconds.

We had materials for drawing, writing, and making books, and there were always books of photographs around. At some point in each semester, after talking with each student about what he liked to take pictures of and what difficulties he was having, I made suggestions about what he might try next.

One of the more difficult tasks was to persuade the children of the eloquence of their rough photographs. They hadn't seen anything like the pictures they were about to take, not in subject matter, tonal range, or surface texture. The portraits they admired were slick album covers of Hank Williams or Dolly Parton; they liked the idyllic landscapes they saw in seed catalogues. But if my words did not always convince them of their gifts, they were able to encourage one another.

As they became more comfortable with the camera, I wanted them to expand their ideas about picture-making, while staying close to the people and places they felt most deeply about. I asked them to photograph themselves, their families, their animals and their community, and to think about stories they might make with photographs. When they made self-portraits, they discovered that they could be the subjects of their own photographs, and could change themselves into whatever characters they chose to create.

One day, while I was staring out the window of my workspace trying to make a plan for the upcoming year, I recalled with cinematic clarity something that had happened at the house of one of my students. Charles was lying on his stomach while his big brother Johnny tied him up, wrists-to-ankle, in the manner of a pig about to be slaughtered. I later asked Johnny and Charles to reenact the scene so I could photograph it for the series *Johnny's Story.* The children in Kentucky often enacted such scenes. For them the whole natural world was a playground and, as in dreams, their play easily crossed borders between animals and humans, between life and death. I saw them seeing a complete and fantastical existence, and I wanted to find a photographic method to match their vision.

I decided to ask the children to photograph their dreams or fantasies. In order to free up the class for their intensely personal and often frightening dreams, we shut ourselves in the darkroom, sat on the floor, and told each other our scariest dreams. The photographs the children took afterwards broke new ground for many of them — and for me. The children seemed not to separate their waking and sleeping worlds, as adults do, and as in dreams ordinary objects became magical vehicles.

Scott Huff hadn't had any luck with his pictures up to then. Now he strode triumphantly into my room with his roll of dream pictures. They would be good, he said, if only he could develop them right. His hands trembled as he agitated the developing tank, but there were no problems, and a fine series of pictures —*A Flying Dream*— resulted.

Allen Shepherd had a fight with his best friend, Ricky Dixon. He and Ricky had swapped knives and Allen felt Ricky had shortchanged him. They refused to speak to one another until one night Allen dreamed that he killed Ricky. He decided to make a photograph of Ricky dead, his body draped in the fork of a tree. He asked Ricky to pose for him. In the course of getting the photograph done, the two boys made up.

I dreamt I killed my best friend, Ricky Dixon. —Allen Shepherd

I took a picture of myself with the statue in the backyard. —Janet Stallard

I am lying on the back of my old horse. — Russell Akeman

My space-ship was taking off. — Scott Huff

The planes were crashing on my head. — Scott Huff

I asked my sister to take a picture of me on Easter morning. — Ruby Cornett

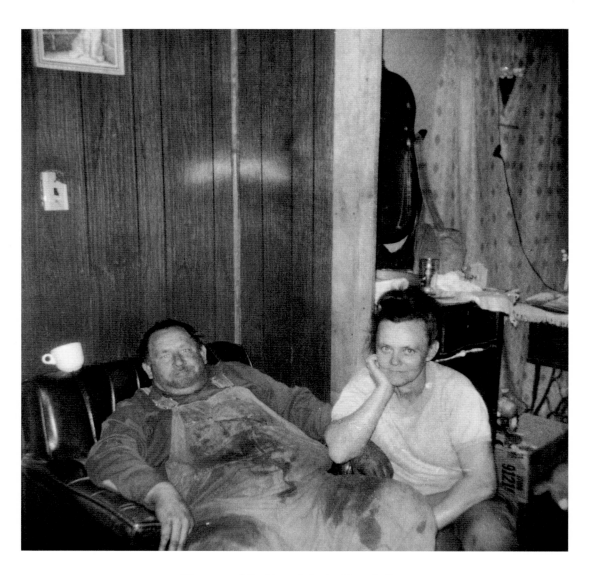

Mommy and Daddy — Martha Campbell

Miners going home at the end of the shift — Ruby Cornett

The women hugging after church — Darlene Watts

Self-portrait with the picture of my biggest brother, Everett, who killed himself when he came back from Vietnam — Freddy Childers

My daddy is measuring our hog. — Joy Ingram

With the first roll of film Denise Dixon took, I saw that she had
a distinctive and original sense of composition. Unlike some of the other
children, she never ran out of ideas. I visited her home several times.
She had set up her room as an oversized dollhouse, with stark white walls
and a few posters of animals and family portraits. On the bureau, the night
table and the bed, she had created tableaux with her dolls — just as in
her photographs where she made up fantasies involving her twin brothers
Philip and Jamie. The meticulous arrangement of her room and the
deliberate way she dressed were reflected in the care she took in composing
her photographs. When I asked her to document her Thanksgiving dinner,
she took a picture of the whole turkey on a platter resting on a bare
Formica table. She included only what was essential.

Denise worked with me from the fourth through the sixth grade.
In the seventh grade she became a cheerleader and basketball player. She
took fewer pictures. Finally she told me she wanted to quit photography
class. She offered no explanation, she had simply lost interest.

During those years, I fell in love with many of the kids. They were
my companions. Once, Denise and I talked for hours, stretched out on
her bed, about her dreams and premonitions. We were like accomplices in
a secret game. We knew, as photographers, that sometimes we had to trick
adults into letting us take the pictures we wanted.

I couldn't push Denise to continue. I realized I was trying to hold
on to a brief period of her life that she had let go of. Her expressiveness
with the camera was a moment in her childhood. She would have to
become aware of her abilities in some other way and consciously try to
become a photographer, if she was to go beyond her instinctual eloquence
with a camera. Maybe she would pick up the camera again; maybe she
would express herself by other means.

I am Dolly Parton. — Denise Dixon

Phillip and Jamie are creatures from outer space in their space-ship. — Denise Dixon

I am the girl with the snake around her neck. — Denise Dixon

My brother the mud monster — Denise Dixon

Self-portrait reaching for the Red Star sky — Denise Dixon

Johnny's Story

As I became an active participant in the community, I decided to make biographies of some of the people I had grown close to. While working in different settings with different people, I became conscious of the effect of context on the images. I started using words, my own and the subjects', to anchor the pictures. I put my photographs together with transcriptions of their life stories, and sometimes with their snapshots, to create multi-dimensional portraits. Johnny was one of my students.

Well, I've got five sisters and two brothers. Charles and Diane live with Mommy and me. My oldest sister, Hazel, she's married to Dewey and runs a flea market beside the road, and Doc Mare, my other brother, we call him Bubby, he's married and got hisself a job. Solouis, we call her Sissy, she's got a job. She's got two kids. My other sister, Clara, she's got a baby and one on the way. She's married and she lives on the road in a car. It's a white station wagon with brown stripes, and Joyce Ann she stays with my older sister that owns that flea market. That is all there is to tell. Oh, Mommy has to go to the doctor probably tomorrow to have some gall stones taken out. Yesterday that woman we rent off of came and told Mommy to lock our bikes when she goes in the hospital, so we won't be on the road. Mommy says she ain't going to go to the hospital.

Mommy's trying to get Joyce Ann to come home. Joyce Ann won't come home because of her boyfriend, Freddy. He comes to see her and takes her to the drive-in. Mommy's going to call Bobby Polly, the welfare worker, and Joyce Ann's going to be put in a foster home, like I was almost. She's fifteen.

My favorite sisters are Sissy and Clara. I wish Clara would get a divorce from Zinzel because he's going to beat her to death. We're all like the same person, except we're different. We look alike in the face. We all have Mommy's eyes. They're real little. We have fingers alike — crooked little fingers. We've got long toes. We almost have the same color hair. Charles' is brown and blond mixed together. Mine is brown and Diane's is brown and has got a little blond in it. I'm tall and Charles is short. But we're all thin and have long arms, long legs. I play with Charles the most. I taught him how to swim.

Johnny and Charles fighting

I tied milk jugs under his arms and threw him out into the middle of the creek.
He started floating and I taught him how to throw his arms down to hold him up.
We've got a little road built out there on the hill. I build toys. I found an old truck
in the creek with no wheels, and about a month later I found wheels and put them
together. Now we have a coal truck, a hot rod car, a rig with two trailers, one
hauls coal, one hauls logs. Instead of hauling logs in the log truck, we use plastic
pipes, and act like it's hauling culverts to put in the road.

Sometimes Diane and I get along like I get along with Charles. She wanted
a tape player for her little tape for Christmas. Mommy bought her one. She went
into debt, sold her antenna and boosters. Diane ain't hardly played it none.
Now she wants a pair of roller-skates to get her neck broken. These big rich people
throw away brand-new stuff they don't want, like a brand-new ashtray, and Diane
finds it and gets it. Brand-new stuff that comes right out of the store.

Bubby, the oldest one, lives up here in Jerimar and Grandma up here in
Eoli. Aunt Ruth lives at Dayton, Ohio, and Uncle Herbert, he's dead. Cancer
killed him. One time he was working for somebody when he was about twelve and
he was cutting a juice wire. When he jerked back, he cut his eye ball right through.
He just pulled the wire out and went on. I got a picture of him holding me in
his arms. I was a little baby. Aunt Margy lives down below Lloyd Brown's store,
over in the holler. That's all the kin I've got. Uncle Fusten, he lives over there in
Bell County. He jumped on some men for liquor and they shot him, right there
in the gut. He didn't die. They put him in the hospital and he couldn't pay his
bill. They sued him and he didn't have nothing. His wife left him because he was
nothing but a drunkard.

We used to live on Kingdom Come Creek. That was the best time of my life.
There were a lot of wild animals there. I remember the night that Daddy heard
something squalling. Sounded like a man trying to kill a woman. Daddy shone
a big old spot-light out and there were two big black panthers killing our hogs,
Johnny and Charlie, named after Charles and me. Those two black panthers had
the hogs' heads stuck in their mouths. Daddy just reared back and "Pow, pow!"
Mommy had the 30/30. Mommy'd shoot that gun like she was shooting a BB gun,
and Daddy had a thirty-eight and just sat there and killed those panthers, one at

a time. Buddy, we had good times. I was ten years old when I moved from Kingdom Come to Bell County. After we moved I never saw panthers no more.

I had the best family in the world until then. Every time something happened to me, I told them about it. One time Bubby was down there fishing and caught a red eye. It was a little thin fish. Bubby jerked it and it came back and hit Diane in the face. I remember when Dewey would wade the Kentucky River just to see Hazel.

Then they sent Daddy to prison. They gave him ten years, but then the judge decided to cut it down to five. He got out now. His parole is up and he's a free man. We saw him once up in Turkey Creek. He was in a big black limo. He must be rich.

When they put Daddy in jail, they let him out of the cell for Mommy to cut his hair. We got to see him a couple of times when he was there. Diane got to go in the jail cell and me and Charles, but Mommy never did. They were afraid she'd sneak something to him. He told Mommy if he didn't hurry up and get out, he was going to kill hisself. About a month later they sent him to LaGrange prison. He stayed a year and two months there. He wrote Mommy a ten-page letter. That made a man out of him because before he got sent to prison he always had a big mouth. You had to play shut-mouth down in prison or you'd get your brains beaten in. We've still got the letter. It's ten different papers — all different colors on each one of the papers. Mommy reads them about once a year. She just sits there and reads them to herself. I can't read so I don't know what they say. I asked Diane to read them to me the other day, but she won't because she likes to play old Missy. My Daddy got put in jail in 1975. We got the letter in 1976. That's the last we heard from him.

When I went into the jail cell, it felt like being a prisoner. Daddy and his buddy were in the last jail cell next to the stairs, next to a big old cell with a lot of guys in it who had committed crimes. His buddy that was in there with him had rabbit in his feet. Every time they would take him down to the trail, he'd get loose from the cops and take for the river. Life would be happy for me if Daddy would ever come back to us. When I get older, if anybody's trying to break my family up, I'll kill them. I know I will.

Charles, hog-tied

Charles and the quilts

Johnny and Charles in the yard

Johnny watching television

Johnny's house

Clara's baby

Johnny and Charles before Christmas

Alicia and her son in their tarpaper house

Colombia 1982–1985

Much as I might have wanted to, I would never become a mountain woman. So reluctantly, after seven years in Kentucky, I moved on. I wanted to work in another mountain community, this time outside of the country, so I went to Latin America. I didn't know if the way I had taught and photographed in Kentucky could be translated to another culture. My idea was that by working away from my native language, I would be forced to rely on my visual skills.

For nearly two years I taught and photographed in Ráquira, a small village in a cool, dry valley on the western spine of the Colombian Andes. Most of my students lived in the mountains above the town and rose before dawn to tend the crops and cattle that would occupy them for their entire lives. I shared what might be called the last year of their childhood.

At first the children had difficulties with the camera. Instead of framing someone's face, as they intended, they would often photograph just the knees or feet. It took me awhile to understand that since there were no windows in the mountain huts where they slept, and since they watched television rarely if at all, the idea of "framing" was utterly foreign to them; they had never seen their surroundings *through* anything. I asked them to carry around a piece of paper with a hole in it and look through it at everything they came upon. Within a couple of weeks, they had no problems using the viewfinder.

Toward the end of my project, on a trip to Bogotá, I was intro-duced to Alicia Vásquez by a mutual friend who was helping rebuild her house. Alicia was twenty-eight and a single mother of three boys. She lived in Barrio Luis Alberto Vega, a squatters' settlement constructed on land claimed from one of the steep Andean slopes towering over the eastern and western sides of Bogotá.

After she had put her children to bed, Alicia and I sat around in the candlelight while she told stories of her life. Her sensitivity and the acuteness of her perceptions drew me to her. Her storytelling became richly detailed as she relived her childhood.

I began to feel that Alicia's story was crucial to any non-Colombian's understanding of the pictures I had taken or those of my students. It also seemed clear that her narrative needed to be "illustrated" in order to ground the magical tone of her storytelling in the historical and contemporary reality of Colombia. The visual and verbal had to be equal.

My camera, however, made Alicia uncomfortable. In fact, she dreamed about being chased by a lens — a lens that felt to her like the Evil Eye. I turned my thoughts and plans to photographing her neighbors and other Colombians living in circumstances similar to her childhood years in the valley of Cauca and her present home in Barrio Luis Alberto Vega. The result was a book called *Magic Eyes: Scenes from an Andean Girlhood,* a narrative that weaves my own and my students' pictures through the story of Alicia's life.

What follows is an excerpt of this book.

The Invasion

Our landlady was a little old lady who drank a lot. Her real name was Concepión de Granados but we all called her Conchita. She called my brother Miguelito "Wheat Roll" because he was fat and brown. On Fridays she went out drinking with all the men who lived in the house. When they got home at dawn, they helped Conchita climb the stairs to her room. Then they went home to fight with their women.

Nine of us families lived downstairs and Conchita lived on the second floor. The room we rented was tiny — ten by nine feet — but we squeezed in two beds, a little table, a chair, and Mama's sewing machine. Our only decoration was a mirror used by the women who came to be fitted for their dresses, and a picture of Our Lady of Mount Carmel.

The house was ugly. Conchita wanted the floor waxed and shined but you couldn't, it was too rotten. The walls were so damp that if you put the bed next to the wall the mattress would turn moldy. We each had one day to wash. No one else could wash even a sock that day. There was one bathroom for all of us.

Some of the people were good. Some weren't. Some left the bathroom dirty and blamed the others. Some stole clothes or food and dumped their garbage in other people's rooms. One girl, Luz Elena, stole underwear, pots, and spoons. She was unpleasant.

When my stepfather Raúl came home drunk, he'd turn up the radio loud. The neighbors would start insulting us and shouting at Raúl to turn it off and let them sleep. Conchita de Granados would have to get up and quiet everyone down.

One time Raúl got into it with a guy next door. This guy worked. I don't know where he worked, but he left early every morning and came back after dark. He lived just on the other side of the wall from us. And like always Raúl came home and turned up the radio and woke everybody up.

Well, one night this guy was in a bad mood. He woke up and shouted, "God damn it! Let me sleep!" And he went to get Conchita, who tripped and rolled down the stairs drunk. Raúl came out and split the guy's head and it all ended at the police station. We slept through most of it. We finally woke up crying. It was time to move.

Mama had heard about a new barrio de invasión, *a squatters' settlement, named after the only woman military hero in Colombia's history, Policarpa Salavarrieta. Policarpa had run messages between Bolívar and his men. When she was only twenty-one, the Spaniards captured her. She was handed over to a firing squad and shot in the back—the method used by the Spaniards to execute traitors. "Miserable people!" she shouted to the crowd that gathered to watch her die. "I pity you. How different your lives would be if you knew the price of liberty. But it's not too late: watch and don't forget this lesson: I am a woman and young, but I have more than enough strength to meet my death—and a thousand more."*

People who didn't have roofs over their heads—and there were hundreds of thousands of them in Bogotá—or people like Mama, who wanted to build something of their own instead of renting a tiny room with no light—organized themselves to invade empty land to build houses out of whatever they could find. You had to do it quickly because in a few hours the police might come to knock down the houses and arrest everybody. Then they elected a government. They built a water system. They stole electricity from the light poles around them. The squatters knew that the longer they stayed and the more permanent the structure they could make, the more chance they had of hanging on. The law said the police had thirty days to remove them if they didn't have the right papers, but even then the police could take it up with the judge and get a new order to kick them out.

People resisted; some people were killed. Sometimes people from other barrios came to help. They'd make a human chain around the land to keep the police out. It was hard. The police destroyed lots of invasiónes. *Gradually the city government had to accept them. Where else were all these people going to live?*

Mama thought she'd take a chance and invade a new section of Policarpa along with forty new families. We might lose everything, but at least we'd try. We'd just gotten everything together when a neighbor asked Mama if she knew the organizers were communists. She said no.

We were raised Catholic. Even to say the word "communism" was a sin. Mama went to the priest and confessed that she'd committed the mortal sin of wanting to live in a communist barrio. The priest said she must not do that, not for all the money in the world, and that a person who was baptized Catholic had to follow the teachings

of the church, that she should run away from communism like Satan runs away from the cross, that communism was Satan himself. She was convinced. She said she didn't want to jump into the flames of Hell. We were doing fine on our own; why should we get involved with communists? Then even God wouldn't touch us. But the rents kept going up and everything got more expensive. Mama started working harder, sleeping two or three hours a night. When she got even more work, she took pills to keep her awake around the clock. She got so hooked that when we finally did move to Policarpa, she couldn't sleep right for four years.

We were still living in Conchita's house when a traveling salesman rented a room there. He was from the south, from near our valley, so we got on fine. He invited us out for Chirstmas Eve and we all had a great time. The salesman mentioned he had joined an organization called Provivienda and they were going to assign him a parcel of land in a new barrio in Policarpa. He was going to invade next week. Why didn't we join up too? Mama told him that frankly she was afraid. "Are the organizers communists?"

"Of course they're communists. The communists are the ones who help the people. But they don't force you to become a communist if you don't want to be one."

He was a good and honest man and Mama says she always pays attention to honest people. But still she couldn't go. She said she felt like a hand was holding her back. The salesman insisted that we visit him in the Charles de Gaulle barrio, which was named after the day they invaded it, the twentieth of July, the day de Gaulle arrived in Colombia. Mama made excuses; she lied. She told him she was very sick.

"Look, María," he said, "one day they'll throw you out on the street, and then you'll have to deal with the situation yourself because I'm not going to beg you anymore. If you're tough enough to work twenty-four hours a day, what's so hard about making a home of your own?"

Then, just like the salesman predicted, our situation got worse. Javier, my older brother, lost his job. Conchita de Granados raised our rent by fifty pesos, which was a lot of money then. So Mama joined Provivienda, the squatters' organization, along with some other women. Now that Raúl didn't always come home, she made her own decisions. After the last Provivienda meeting before the scheduled invasion, Conchita de Granados evicted us.

The other squatters said they'd get the wood for our new house. Just bring an old bed and mattress, they said.

We moved into the community center built by the first group of squatters in Policarpa. Five years earlier they had invaded the empty fields around Hortua Hospital, where later the government said it had planned to build a new hospital. All those families in one building, baby bottles all over the place, common meals cooked in enormous pots—people started getting sick. They trucked in milk and groceries and we had to stand guard and when the doctors came from Hortua Hospital they said we had to build real houses or there'd be an epidemic.

It was Good Friday in 1966. The shacks were all made with sticks and paper and cloth. We set up poles for the sides; we had tarpaper for the walls and tin for the roof. Each house was a black box you put beds in. Javier wrote our name in crayon on each board, so when everything was unloaded we'd know where it belonged.

At noon, just as we were about to eat lunch, the organizers gave the order to invade the field in front of the hospital. They had already torn down the fence around it. Some of us went over the Hortua Hospital wall, and the others got in through the farm next door. We didn't all go in at one time, just a few through here, a few through there. I was so scared I walked like I was on stilts.

Raúl and some of his friends put their shoulders under the corners of the black box and raised it carefully. Now our black box had legs. Everyone ran into the field, carrying the house frames and setting them down in blocks. When Mama and I got there, Javier, Raúl and a gentleman named Luis Alberto Vega had set up our house and the things were already inside. Luis Alberto Vega was not a leader or anything, just a sympathizer. He got killed on Easter Sunday, the day of the battle.

They set the shack down on a floor of grass, like a green carpet. Our little shack made the earth into a beautiful rug. When you wanted to open the door or let the sun in, you rolled the tarpaper around a stick and threw it on the roof. Then you had a bright house without windows or anything. So in fifteen minutes it was done.

By one-thirty on Easter Sunday, when the police showed up, we were ready. Protestors and help arrived from everywhere. The organizers gave orders for the women and children not to leave. I lit a fire and boiled water to throw at the police.

The president of Colombia, Guillermo León Valencia, who was so unpopular he had to declare a state of siege to keep himself in power, watched the gun battle from the terrace of the hospital.

The army surrounded the barrio. They made holes in the wall around the hospital to let the cavalry in. The soldiers were shivering from the cold. The rice and flour merchants brought trucks full of food and blankets for the squatters. The police wouldn't let them through. But when the shift changed, the new soldiers were careless. The trucks drove right through the holes in the hospital wall.

The orders were that if they attacked us, we should throw rocks.

Suddenly there was olive green everywhere. The police came and then the cavalry and you could hear shots. The families below us were being beaten and their houses ripped apart. Mama went to help them. Javier was on the hill waving a flag made out of a white sheet and he was helping to carry the rocks the men were throwing at the police. I stayed in the house with Miguelito so nothing would happen to him.

"Even if they knock the house down," Mama said, "don't you leave."

The bed was set up in the middle of the room. Miguelito was playing in the bed and he reached out to grab a toy from the ground and just then the cavalry galloped by and all of a sudden the point of a bayonet sliced through the tarpaper and just missed his hand.

The adults had a supply of rocks ready. As soon as she heard the first shots, Mama got afraid. But she ran ahead anyway, and when that tremendous battle began she said she forgot all about us and everything. The only thing that mattered was to attack because the police were firing at them. Some of the kids were collecting rocks, and there were rocks flying every which way, and they drove the police back twice.

It was worse on the opposite end — away from the hospital — where they sent in the cavalry. Everybody had thick branches with very sharp points, and balls of rags, tied together with wire and asphalt and drenched in gasoline. So when the cavalry charged, they lit their torches and poked them under the horses' flanks and the horses threw their riders way up in the air. When the cavalrymen fell, they lost their weapons and ran, but the people didn't just stand there looking at them; they kept pelting them with rocks and throwing hot water on them.

The police started shooting through the houses. The organizers shouted to the men to leave, so the police could see there were only women and children inside. They shot one man who'd built his house above us and they kicked him and dragged him around in front of us. What finally calmed things down in the end was a rain shower at four in the afternoon.

They say we live in the most Catholic country in the world. It was Easter Sunday and every family had an altar in their shack. The goons went in anyway and after the battle the statues of the saints were still there, crushed in the mud by the policemen's horses.

They brought in police cars to take away the wounded on both sides. They said none of the policemen died but I myself saw a dead one. They took Luis Alberto Vega to his house because he didn't die immediately. Two children died later, I heard. They took a lot of us to jail. The police said: "Tell us who brought you here and we'll give you a house to live in." But we were ready for that. We said: "It was need that brought us here; we came here because we don't have money to pay rent and the land-lords threw our things into the street." The police said we were dirty commies but they let us go.

We held Luis Alberto Vega's wake in the community center. They wouldn't let anyone leave to bury the body in a cemetery so we buried him under Twenty-Sixth Street. The police had to be careful after that, because word got out that they'd been so cruel.

Those were good times. We were young. Every morning I'd pull back the blanket, trying not to uncover Javier's brown feet next to my head. I stepped out of bed and looked at the picture of Saint Lucy pasted to the headboard. The beautiful saint with brown wavy hair and blue eyes would protect me until I climbed into bed again. I walked quickly, trying not to trip over one of the trenches Mama had dug in the dirt floor. The floor turned into mud when it rained unless, when the shower began, Mama dug a trench to let the water flow down the mountain.

We played hide-and-seek in Antonio Nariño school. The playground was tiny. I learned to draw the map of Colombia. Almost all of us lived in Policarpa, but when we enrolled we had to lie about that. If we said we were living in the squatters' camp,

they would say we were bad students and expel us. I used to say that I lived in a barrio way in the north.

But we were happy even if the floor was muddy or high grass grew up in our house. It was a wonderful place to play. Since we didn't have water we had to walk three blocks to the public faucets and carry it back in buckets. Mama wanted to build something in brick right away, so she began washing clothes, sewing, doing a thousand things.

We took turns standing guard. We had to make sure no strangers came in at night. If anybody saw anything, they called out, and the first one to reach the alarm, rang it. The kids did guard duty, too. We walked and walked and listened to the adults talk about a lot of things. That the women should be more active; that we had to go talk with the government to demand services in the barrio . . . so they'd legalize our status fast.

We'd heard a new invasión *was planned. We understood that housing was very important, and because we already had a place to live we wanted to help others. At three in the morning the leaders went from house to house like an alarm clock. "Sister, do you want to come with us and help our brothers and sisters take their land?"*

Nuevo Quindío was hilly, and colder than Policarpa. We had to go around the mountain to avoid the police. To sleep we had to dig up the sod in the pasture and wrap ourselves in it. We put the children between two adults so they wouldn't freeze.

They caught Javier when he was bringing food. You could get two to twenty months for invading. They put him in the district jail. They told him we were subversives, but we didn't even know what the word meant. I knew only that my brother was my brother and Mama was Mama. We were raised to go after what we wanted. We learned a lot about justice and injustice. We had proof that to get a piece of land you had to fight for it. No matter what.

—Alicia Vásquez

India 1989 – 1990

When I looked at the beautiful pictures by photographers Raghubir Singh, Mitch Epstein and others, India seemed a place more visually rich than any I had seen, a country where exquisitely composed images would fall into my hands. In Colombia I had learned that by staying close to one family's story, it was possible to create a context for pictures that might otherwise be seen as exotic. I was interested in finding out if, by working with a small group of people, I could organize and articulate meaning in the small, layered world of village India.

Vichya is a village in the State of Gujarat, northwest of Bombay. According to local traditions, the settlement originated five hundred years ago, in the aftermath of a war between two princely brothers. Today, just as five centuries ago, Vichya is comprised of family or caste groupings in clusters of mud houses. The surrounding country looks like one vast sprawling city — though "city" is not quite the word. "City" conveys the density of it, but not the linkages. Two thousand people live within the walls of Vichya. Inside, there are small fields for the cultivation of rice and spices, and people — people everywhere.

My advisors were Jhivanbhai, the village barber, and his daughter Usha. In the interest of impartiality, they suggested that I choose students on the basis of a simple test. The next day a long line of children snaked out of the barber's yard onto the sandy road linking the village to the highway. One by one I asked the children to look through the camera, identify what they saw, and tell me what they wanted to take pictures of, and why. Most of them said the same thing: they wanted to photograph the gods.

I asked Dasrath, the cobbler's son, to show me a photograph. He pointed to the front of the barber's house, which was adorned with fanciful images of Hanuman, the winged monkey god, and Krishna, the beautiful blue man-god. Dasrath thought the camera was a machine that could manufacture any image conjured in his mind, just as easily as it could record the things he saw in front of his eyes.

It was impossible to make the bamboo roofs of the mud houses light-tight, so in the barber's front yard we started building a brick and concrete darkroom with a tin roof. Alongside this structure, in exchange for his customary fee of fifty kilos of rice per year, the barber continued to give haircuts and shaves to the men of the village.

When the darkroom was ready, we planted our ritual basil plant (sacred to Krishna) to provide the "black house," as the darkroom was called, with an auspicious beginning. Students and parents gathered for the opening ceremony; the students spoke about what they had learned so far, and recited prayers.

From the most enthusiastic children I chose an equal number of those who attended school and those who, because they had to work in the fields, did not. My class had a wide representation of different castes. My students included members of the farmer caste as well as professional castes such as shopkeepers and barbers, and the lowest caste — the Harijans (Untouchables).

My first task was to show my students how the camera really worked, and what it could do. I set up a crude portrait studio on the front porch of my house. I asked each child to sit down and look into the lens while I took a Polaroid photograph, so they could see a negative and a positive image right away, and take these home with them. I was struck by the intensity of their gazes as they looked into the camera for the first time.

Tidi and her Harijan neighbors

Every time I walk by the pond, I pray to the gods to make me strong — like a piece of wood on fire.

When I'm twenty years old I'll beat all of the boys with a stick. I'll work in the fields — whatever work I can get, wherever I can get money.

My birthplace is Vichya, in this house. When I was born, the old woman Nathi came to help, and Lauro Doshi too. I don't remember anything, but my mother said the birth was quick.

I'm a member of the Vaghri caste; we make wine. When no one is in the house, I fill a glass with the wine and drink it quietly. We beg for food — like the flute players. My mother is going to beg for food today in this village; I'm going to another.

I have three sisters and one brother. My brother's name is Sabu. Laxmi is my eldest sister. The others are Paku and Tidiben. When I was two years old my father died. I don't know how. My brother and sister-in-law are dead too. It happened when my brother was drinking. He hit his wife in the throat with an iron bar and killed her. Then he hung himself.

I only dream about elephants. I'm afraid because the elephants' legs are so thick that if they come down on me, I'll be crushed.

I like the village very much because I have many friends here. If I'm in the city where will I go and find my friends? I'll get lost somewhere. If there are two markets next to each other, I'll get lost right there. In the village I can go out, play wherever I want and come back to my house.

My house is better than the whole world. No one can say anything to me there. In another house they could say I'm a thief and beat me.

— Pratap, Vaghri (Wine Maker Caste)

I have a mommy, father, two brothers, and three sisters. One brother is married and the other is going to marry. My father laughs a lot, but I don't like him when he beats us. My small brother and cousin are at home. One younger brother and sister got smallpox right after they were born. I was very small then, but I remember they were suffering from fever. My mother prayed to the god of smallpox and he appeared in her dreams. He told her not to use the medicines and when the children were well again, that she should take sweets to the temple to thank him for sparing their lives. So we fed my brother and sister, but didn't give them medicines. When they died, we buried them on the roadside and marked the grave with a red cloth. I can't find it now. The sweepers must have taken it away.

I like to wash clothes and dishes, fetch water, and go to work in the fields. I like to wear nice new clothes and make myself up. I like to play with tops and fly kites and knock the others' kites out of the sky with a bamboo stick.

But I had to leave my studies because of the housework. Anyhow, soon we have to marry. I'll be happy then. My husband will get me a scooter. I'll get on it and wander. I might be sad. It depends if I have a nice house. I'd like a cement bungalow and a good husband. But I won't know until I'm married whether the house is nice or bad. I'd choose a man who is a homely, quiet fellow, so I can beat him. I'd like him to have a mustache and wear trousers and a shirt. I want sons, as many as God wants to give me—two, three, or four. I'll play with my children and scold them when they're mischievous. When I'm older I'll look after my husband's house.

I get enough food to eat—even during the drought. We went to the city then and lived in our uncle's house for six months. All the Harijans went. My father did construction work. My mother helped him and washed dishes, but I'd like to go to school.

As long as God wants me to be a Harijan, I like being a Harijan, but no other village people except relatives will come to our house to eat. Like Samju can't come to my house. But Hansi's a Harijan, so she can eat with me. When there is a wedding, the bride's family thinks their house will be spoiled if we enter it, so we sit outside and eat. I feel bad about that, but sometimes it's better.

Dreams come from God—from all the gods. My grandmother dreamed that the god of death had come to take her. She told him, "I will not come with you. This is not the time." The god of death placed his hand over her nose and mouth. When she woke up, her mouth and nose were swollen. Whenever I have a dream and get scared, I fall off my kotla. *Hansi had a dream that she and I went to God's house and he gave us necklaces and prayed with us.*

— Tidi, Harijan (Untouchable Caste)

I saw my father only once that I remember. I was still young. His name is Kesav and he is as old as a grandfather. My sister stays with my uncle in the village of Hutipura, where my father lives. She works for my auntie. My features are like my mother's; my sister looks like my father. I don't like my father. He's an opium addict.

When I was very small, my uncle brought me here. I sleep with my grandmother Surejma, who lives alone in one room. When she's not here, I stay with my uncle. I have seven uncles and seven aunties.

A long time ago, my mother and I came here to Vichya for a ceremony. As we walked back home afterwards, my mother started picking up mustard seeds that had fallen during the harvest. On the ground she found silver coins, Laxmi coins. I don't know how much money it was. When my mother got home, she put the silver coins in the water pot and buried it to hide it from my father. When he heard about this, my father demanded that she give him the coins. She refused. At night when she was sleeping he sat on her neck and choked her to death. Then he dug up the pot. But when he went to take the money, the pot was filled with water. It's still in the ground. Then he went through the house and took all my mother's gold and silver ornaments. Now when he comes here to get opium, he calls for me, but I don't go.

One boy from Daine village came to look at me for marriage. I cried when the girls told me he'd come. My life will be nothing after I marry. I'll just have to work.

— Sajjan, Koli Patel (Farmer Caste)

I got married two months ago. It was a nice day. We all went to my wife's village on a tractor. No one danced, but people sang. I enjoyed it.

I married Galli from Vasna near Dhodal. My sister married a fellow from Vasna and when we visited her I saw Galli fetching water. I had no idea that I would marry her, but she knew. When I got engaged, Galli's relatives came here to the village. Her father brought me a turban, a letter, and a piece of paper. Then he put a coconut in my hand and brought me a bowl of butter to drink. Her father's a rich man, so she brought lots of money and gold ornaments with her.

Galli wears village skirts and saris. She's tall. Maybe I'll grow to be a tall fellow like her, but short boys get married, too. She's thirteen and I am fourteen. I like her. She's good natured and good looking. I took four or five pictures of her standing by the door. I'd like to bring her to photography class, but she'll feel shy. She doesn't fight with me. She always respects me and when she doesn't, I'll send her away. I slapped her once when she talked against me. She told her parents. I thought my father-in-law would scold me, but he said that if she did anything wrong I should beat her. Eventually I'll go to my father-in-law's place to live. They have a scooter and two cycles over there. I'll need a kid also. I want only one son—no, both, a son and a daughter. I'll name the boy Mahesh and the girl Wendy.

Once we got married, my wife went back to her village. She came back here twice to stay. When she came for Divali holiday, I was sitting outside. I was ready for her—wearing new pants and a new shirt. I have three safari suits for fancy dress. She stayed for fifteen days, so I had to dress nicely all that time.

I don't have any brothers and sisters at home, so I like it when she comes to stay. I have three sisters but they are married. One brother died in an accident and one drowned. He was a lame fellow—neither of his legs worked. When he walked to the fields on crutches, he always passed a dump. One day it was filled with water and he fell into it and drowned.

I dream about my brothers that died, so at night I cover myself with the blanket to keep away the dreams. When my heart beats, the dream comes out. It shouts from the whole body. "I'm coming out," and then it comes out. On Divali I dreamed that I went up to the sun in a balloon. I saw two goats standing on the edge of the sun and they tried to butt me away. We are all dreaming, but in the morning when we open our eyes the dreams are all gone.

Last night I dreamed I had a girl in my pocket.

— Hasmukh, Koli Patel (Farmer Caste)

In cultures where photographs are uncommon, the camera is often used as a means of bestowing respect. The children of Vichya certainly didn't feel their own lives were worthy of pictures. They had few ideas about what they wanted to photograph. The only images, two- or three-dimensional, that they had ever seen were of the gods. By asking them to use the camera as a means of self-expression, I introduced the idea that they could make the pictures they wanted, not just "statues," as they came to call posed, formal frontal photographs.

My recommendation was not popular with everyone. At first some of the adults of the village worried that if they were photographed from the back or the side or in the middle of doing something, their neighbors might laugh. Sometimes people became incensed, but the children, aware of the new power the camera gave them, persisted.

Watching the children, I began to feel as if I too were learning photography for the first time. Once again, the developing tanks, the reels, and the changing bag became magical instruments. When I saw the children standing so straight as they balanced the camera in their hands, I remembered how I felt when I first slung a camera over my shoulder, how it conferred an air of authority, masking my shyness. My students lived in a society whose cardinal virtue was self-effacement; as children and as rural people, they were held in the lowest esteem. But they told me that when they "caught their cameras" and decided what to photograph, they felt proud.

My lame cousin-brother is dressed like saint Sadhu Hari. —Kalu Rupsingh

Hemat left his shoes behind when he went to worship the goddess Chamunda. — Chandu

My cousin-sister is sad because she is poor and her sister is sick. — Chandrakant

Rasik, the lame boy, and Gitendra are squirting water at each other on Holi, but Rasik's water won't come out because it's mixed with cow dung. — Harsa

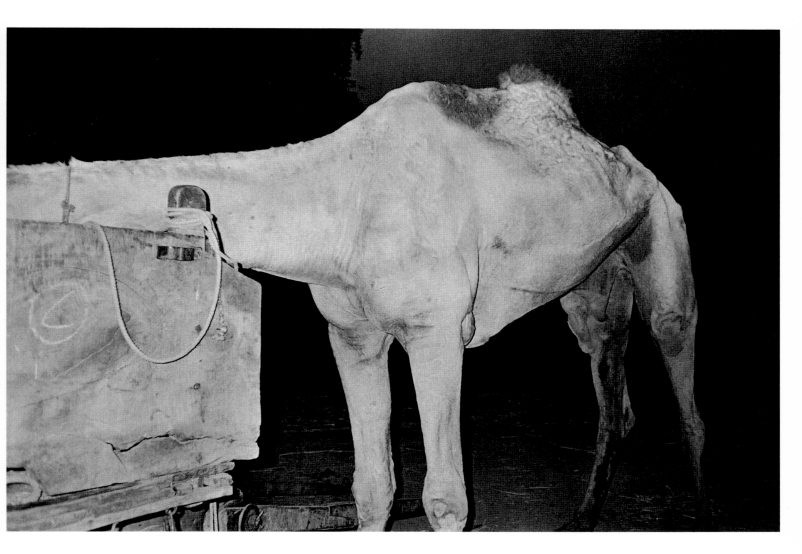

The camel is eating. — Kalu Rupsingh

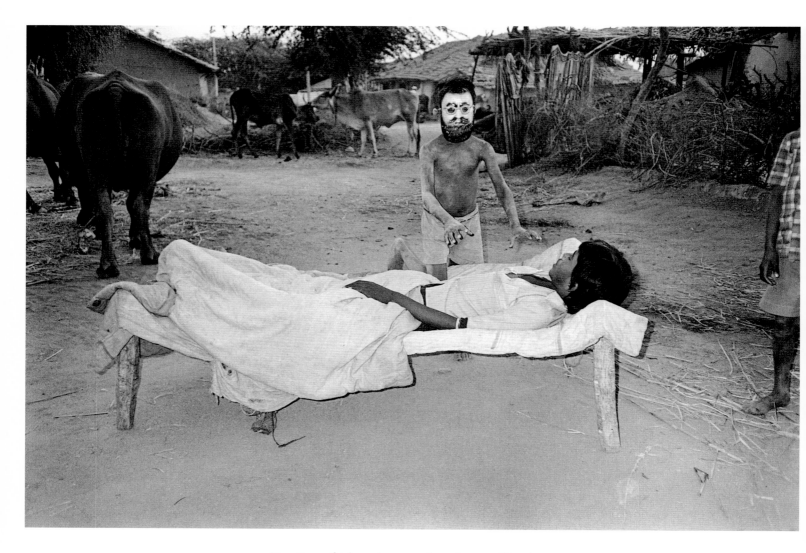

King Ravan frightened me out of my sleep. — Chandu

Chandu's feet are going to crush me. — Kalu Mohanji

My uncle Kashiram is playing with his bow and arrow in the stable. — Kalu Rupsingh

Playing Holi — Harsa

A village girl is shouting for her kite. — Kalu Mohanji

Praying to the gods — Kalu Rupsingh

It was the night before Somchen's wedding and I asked
him not to look at the camera. —Pratap

Saint Bhaataji cut off my hand. — Dasrath

To: Mrs. Wendy Taylor
Chandrakant C. Chauhan
Sainik School Balachadi
India

30th January 1995

Dearest Wendyben,

Hello! How do you do? My praying to God that yourself, your husband, your father and mother would be enjoying the life of New York one of the best cities in the U.S.A.

First of all, I must introduce myself. I am one of the small kids in your group which lived with you in India for most probably six or seven months. I am Chandrakant from India in Gujarat from Vichya village. If you don't remember me than you would remember that day when I had fallen all the negatives hanging on the wire and by this you was very angry.

Now, I am understanding the importance of you, when you came to our village. You talked at that time, when all the boys and girls were called to Jhivanbhai's house. In real, I failed that test. Fortunately I was given chance in place of another boy. Now, I am able to understand why you came to India. It was to see and observe the Indian culture and its traditions. If you want to know more details about Indian culture, how can I help you?

Wendyben, we want you and your husband to come to our village to see all of us. Now Dasrath is doing an engineering course and Chandu and Harsha have got married as you also got married. I am studying and preparing well for my final exam of ninth standard.

Wendyben, we are all regarding you every time and every moment especially when I will see any photo or camera, but after so many years past you haven't faced towards us. All are fine here. Sakuben and her family are very happy. You must not worry about that. Their eldest son got married. They have now a very much settled life. All are happy and praying to God that you must come to see us with your kids, so that we can share love to them also.

Wendyben, I have lots to write but there is a limit of everything. Now my limit comes. I am putting my pen down and hoping that your pen is in your hand as soon as you get this letter. Lots of love to all.

—Chandrakant C. Chauhan

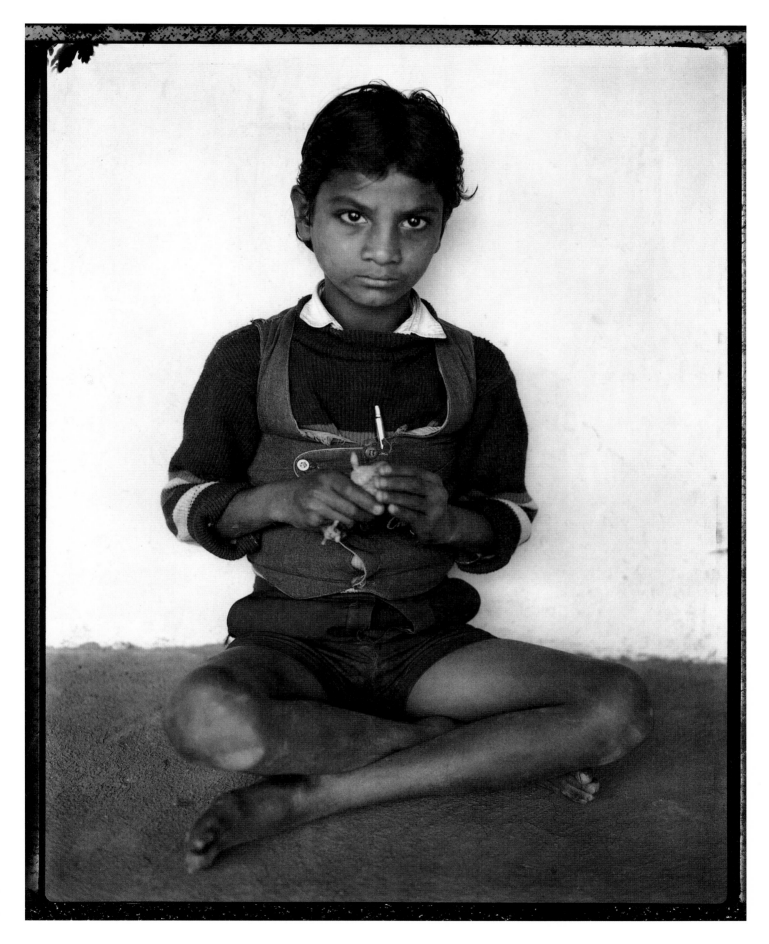

Mexico 1991

In the state of Chiapas, on a hill overlooking the center of the village of
Zinacantán there is a small building that has been outfitted as a classroom.
This was where Antonio de la Torre, a member of the Mayan writers' co-
operative called Sna Jtz-ibajom, taught the reading and writing of Tztotzil
to children in the village. For the past four hundred years, the Tzotzil
Indians, descendants of the Mayans and heirs to their great culture, have
lived in this region alongside the Ladinos, descendants of the original
Spanish explorers.

When I was asked to go to Mexico to create an exhibition to mark
the anniversary of Columbus' arrival in the New World, I decided to go
to Chiapas. I set up photography classes for Ladino children in the town
of San Cristóbal de las Casas, and for Tzotzil children in Zinacantán and
Chamula.

It was one year before the Zapatistas' armed revolt for the cause
of equal rights for Indians. In the Tzotzil communities, taking pictures was
strictly controlled by the local council, who gave or withheld permission as
to what might be photographed. I thought it best not to take any pictures
of my own, and to let my Indian and non-Indian students take photographs. We used Polaroid positive-negative film, which produces a large-
format negative in addition to a positive print. I had misgivings about this
picture-making process — it is slow and deliberate to the point of being
awkward. But it led to more consciously composed pictures, in comparison
to the work of my previous students, who had used simple point-and-shoot
cameras. Yet there was no loss of freshness and spontaneity.

In Zinacantán ten children — five boys, five girls — gathered for
my photography class. Antonio carried in tiny wooden chairs. The girls sat
on one side of the room, the boys on the other.

I showed them postcards by local photographers, images I assumed
they would be familiar with. I asked the children to point out everything

Here is my cousin, Miry, with the skulls and fruit for the Day of the Dead. —Juan Jesús Murillo

they could see in the pictures. They hesitated at first, but as they caught on and started naming things, they began to laugh. Anastasio, a boy wearing an especially bright pink poncho, asked why I was showing them pictures of these people. Were they very good people from whom they must learn how to live? It struck me that the children's concept of images was like their understanding of traditional stories; both images and stories existed to tell moral stories.

As I continued to work in different settings, I noticed the ways in which images were regarded in profoundly different ways from place to place. In India, when the children told me they wanted to take pictures of the gods, I realized that for them there was a more or less automatic connection between their picture-making and their religion. Clearly, the purpose of their photographs was not at all like the repository of secular memories on my parent's library wall.

The Ladino children in Chiapas, however, were familiar with the casual Western concept of pictures as snapshots. After showing them how to open and close the camera and how to look through the viewfinder, I asked them to practice squinting one eye. An earnest dark-haired boy named Juan Jesús had trouble closing one eye, so I put my hand over his left one. "But Señora," Juan Jesús said, "I can't see out of that eye." I noticed the pupil of his eye was white — the eye was blind. "I have an advantage over the others," he said with a laugh.

I wondered why Juan Jesús wanted so badly to take photographs. Was it a kind of compensation for the difficulty he had in seeing? Or was what he saw so distinctive or limited that it was similar to the way a camera sees? Or was he able to see, by using the camera, what he missed with his everyday sight?

Juan Jesús turned out to be one of the best photographers of all the Ladino students. He loved to capture patterns of light falling on his subjects. He also mentioned that when his friends spoke about things they did together, they talked about what they had seen. Juan's eyesight was too poor to pick up these images, so he often felt left out of conversations with his friends, and alienated from their memories. The photographs he made were a way of having a visual memory as rich or richer than his friends'.

The Pro-Pack cameras used by the children had to be focused by adjusting the lens to the proper number of feet or meters to the subject. It is difficult for children to estimate distance, so I measured each child's foot. We calculated how many actual feet made a meter. Then they could pace off the number of feet between them and their subject.

The Tzotzil wanted to create their own ways of working with the camera. They soon informed me that my method of measuring their shoes or feet was not right. With a borrowed machete they cut corn stalks in one meter lengths and used them to measure the distance to their subjects. Some children set up scenes of their friends hoeing fields or gathering flowers. After each shot, they peeled the positive from the negative image; the negatives they placed in plastic buckets to soak in sodium sulfite. The first time I showed them the negatives, they laughed to see themselves as *viejos,* old people (their jet-black hair had gone white). Then they set out to take pictures, ten children running off with corn stalks and plastic buckets clattering, like characters in a ritual play.

When I first asked the Tzotzil children to photograph their dreams or fantasies I was worried that they might be disdainful of the idea. For them, dreams play as important a role in understanding the world as do waking events.

I explained as briefly as I could what we would be doing the next day. They giggled excitedly. *"Fantasías!"* they said, as if both the sound and the idea of the word were funny in a familiar way.

I realized the next day that they knew exactly what I was talking about. They turned up with masks they had made from the gray reverse side of cracker boxes. One was the mask of a jaguar, another of a demon, and another was a devil with horns protruding from the sides of his jaw. The resemblance to figures in Mayan glyphs was striking.

A jaguar is eating chicken. —Salvador Gómez Jiménez

My dog walking in the patio — Teresa López

The phantom — Teresa López

Wolfman and his enemy — Javier Bautista

A boy is playing — pretending he's a clown. — Dolores Gómez Hernández

My sister carrying water — Luis Hernández Gómez

A boy was crushed by a barrel. — Reymundo Gómez Hernández

When I sleep, I see some things, but it's not a dream because I don't know how to dream. When we were sleeping, something came to the house. It made a noise on the roof like someone playing ball. Then I saw it dancing between the rafters, but it was a little fellow. It had a white chest, but its face was all black.

We have animal companion souls — all very different. Some have dogs, cats, jaguars, coyotes and all kinds of animals. The people who have jaguars are the strongest, but the cat is the weakest. The strongest have two or three animal souls — like my father, he has three jaguars.

If someone dies, as God says, we all go to the underworld to pay our sins and then to heaven. I believe there is an Earth Lord that looks like a white person. If he tells us to close our eyes, when we open them, we'll see that we are in another world. If we enter his house, all we can see is cane. No sun gets in. If he tells us, "Sleep with my servant," when we wake up we'll see that we are with serpents. When the dawn breaks, they will turn back into a woman. The Earth Lord has children that are also serpents and because of that we can't kill snakes or the Earth Lord might kill us.

—Nicasio Peréz de la Cruz, Zinacantán

I was born in this place. My parents told me that when I was born and was a baby, they gave me salt, a machete, a notebook and a pencil, so that when I became an adult, I would be a worker and a smart student. I also remember a story when my mother went to wash clothes in the water hole and I fell in. My mother quickly pulled me out so that I wouldn't drown. If she hadn't done this, I wouldn't exist now.

—Sebastián Gómez Hernández, Chamula

The devil is spying on the girls. — Sebastián Gómez Hernández

The river monsters — Javier Bautista

My uncle Mariano is working in the field. — Juan Ricardo Hernández López

The hens are piled up around an altar outside the house. — Sebastián Gómez Hernández

A boy is dressed like a girl. — Sebastián Gómez Hernández

My uncle and his children are thrashing beans. — Marcos Xilón Gómez

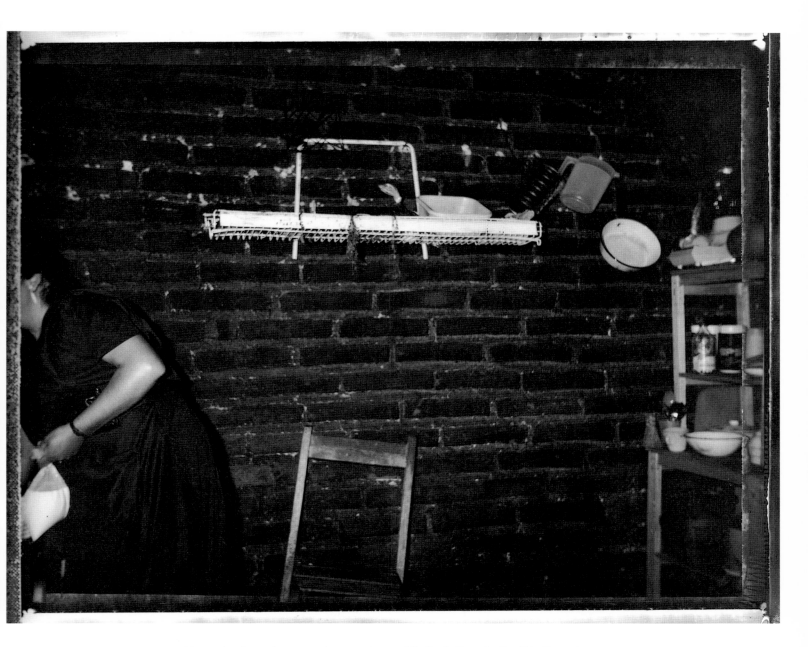

My mother is putting away the groceries. — Gladis de Rosario Bonifáz Guzmán

My father is a masonry contractor. He goes from here to Simójovel, to Cancúc,
to make schools and playing courts. He doesn't take me along because he says I'm only
going to suffer over there. My mother sells pork in the market in front of the statue
of the Virgin of Mercy. I don't like to go with her. She scolds me because I want my
popsicle, my drink and this and that.

— Gladis de Rosario Bonifáz Guzmán, San Cristóbal de las Casas

I dreamed about a magazine and then I saw little squares. A little flower appeared
and at the end a black wave covered it up.

    When you sleep, your soul goes off and everything that happens to it is what
you dream.

    If I remember a dream, I look for an image that reminds me of it and take
a picture of that.

— Benjamín Molino, San Cristóbal de las Casas

It's a mask, a rag and a mop, but I say it's a monster. — Benjamín Molino

A man killing his enemy — Christian Alberto López Medina

My sister is braiding her hair. — Nicasio Peréz de la Cruz

I think that there is something like clouds in my mind. When I imagine a lot of things, the clouds fill up as if it's about to rain.

—Teresa López, San Cristóbal de las Casas

I am the sixth child, but we're many. I think that some weren't born right because they died when they were babies. They only made a small stopover to see the earth. Then they went up to be angels. Those of us who are alive, I don't know how many we are. The oldest is named Domingo and I follow after.

—Dominga Gonzáles Castellanos, Chamula

All my brothers and sisters —Reymundo Gómez Hernández

I think that the backgrounds of small thoughts are white. If I imagine a man, I just place him against a white background but if it's a landscape or a big thought I imagine it in more detail.

—Juan Jesús Murillo, San Cristóbal de las Casas

My father is a chemist and my grandma was a doctor. My sister is studying to be a surgeon. I want to be a doctor like my sister. I resemble my father because he's always in a good mood—just like me.

Vladimir Stálin Becerril Vargas is my complete name. My father read my name and my brothers' and sisters' in a book. My oldest sister is called René, then comes Thalia, and Patria, Maya, Galileo, then I follow and my little brother Bach.

—Vladimir Stálin Becerril Vargas, San Cristóbal de las Casas

The whole family is eating. These are my cousins. — Wendy López Medina

My friends are picking flowers. —Salvador Gómez Jiménez

Sebastian was punished for eight hours. — Dominga González Castellanos

The hens going into the kitchen — Vladimir Stálin Becerril Vargas

The devil is leaving his cave. — Reymundo Gómez Hernández

Ten kilometers by foot into the bush

Seventeen on the way to fetch some water

Poor woman had a baby on her back

Got strike by lightning on the way

To fetch some water

She tried hiding under the trees to save the child

Poor woman had no place to go

Lightning caught her with her child on her back

She ran for help but it was too late

— Sung by Soweto students

South Africa 1992

By now I had become curious to know how things looked to children around the world. I decided to go to Africa, then to an Arab country. I had contacts in South Africa, but I was hesitant to work there because it seemed to offer overly clear divisions between black and white, good and evil. I was concerned that my students' photographs would be mere illustrations of a struggle I presumed I was familiar with. What I hadn't taken into account was the psychological isolation the Afrikaners had inflicted on themselves.

I arrived in Johannesburg in 1992, two years after Nelson Mandela's release from prison, and two years before the National Party, the enforcers of *apartheid,* would cede control of the government to the ANC. Despite these epochal changes, I quickly discovered there was still very little possibility of working with a racially mixed group of children.

I found three different groups to work with: two African and one Afrikaner. One group met at an art center in Soweto. Now and then guards armed with AK-47s patrolled the razor-wire fence. Another group met in an abandoned chicken coop/classroom of the Beauty Botle school in Orange Farm, a squatters' community. In the working-class Johannesburg suburb of Glenesk, the group of Afrikaner children got together at the house of a woman known as Auntie Lorraine.

The black children in Soweto took pictures only in their homes and front yards. They were afraid to shoot outside, they said, because squinting through the viewfinder would narrow their vision and blind them to potential attackers.

The Afrikaner children kept to their homes, too, for fear of the blacks who worked in small factories bordering Glenesk. When the children were asked to take pictures of what they liked and didn't like about their community, all of them, as examples of their dislikes, photographed black people. Most photographed their "nanny girls," the maids who cleaned and cooked in even the poorest white households. Nine-year-old

Nicoline produced a picture of an older black man smiling and holding a shopping bag while he stood outside the fence surrounding her yard. Nicoline had neglected to focus the camera; the sun glinted off the glasses on the black man's blurry face, making him look like an amiable monster. When I asked Nicoline if she had used the camera properly, she replied that she had. Her mother had assured her that the strange blurriness was characteristic of the way that black people appeared in photographs.

In Orange Farm, a new and fast-growing suburb of African refugees from the violence in Soweto and Natal, the children were able to photograph wherever they wanted in their dynamic, makeshift community. One day, however, I was informed that two policemen had confiscated Bafana's camera on the grounds that it was stolen merchandise. When Bafana identified the accusing officers in the underground bunker that served as the waiting room of the local police station, the officers replied that the children would be required to carry letters authorizing them to use the cameras. The children decided to risk going to jail rather than carry the letters. "Blacks have the right to use cameras, too," Flora said, and the others agreed.

The children exhibited their photographs in a gallery in downtown Johannesburg. At the opening party, children from all three groups met for the first time, and saw their photographs enlarged to museum-size format. I had arranged for cameras to be available at the gallery. The kids fingered the straps apprehensively. The Afrikaner students couldn't believe the blacks knew how to take pictures. They thought it best for the blacks to confine themselves to using a few damaged, marginally functional cameras.

John Jackson, an Afrikaner, stood incredulous as he watched Jacob Masilela, a talented photographer from Orange Farm, take a crisp, well-exposed photograph of his companions. I asked Jacob to take some pictures of the exhibition. He posed John looking admiringly at his picture of squatters moving into Orange Farm. It seemed the boys could respect one another as fellow photographers. When I took the final group picture, they threw their arms around one another's shoulders.

What I don't like about where I live — a black man — Nicoline Cuyler

A dream of my sister and her baby — Natasha Prinsloo

My mother catching the ball — Palesa Molahloe

My younger sister going to church — Franklin Monnakqtla

My father playing with the dog — Robert Mbokane

Makhoo, Nombuso and Thuli are looking at the album. —Pamela Zungu

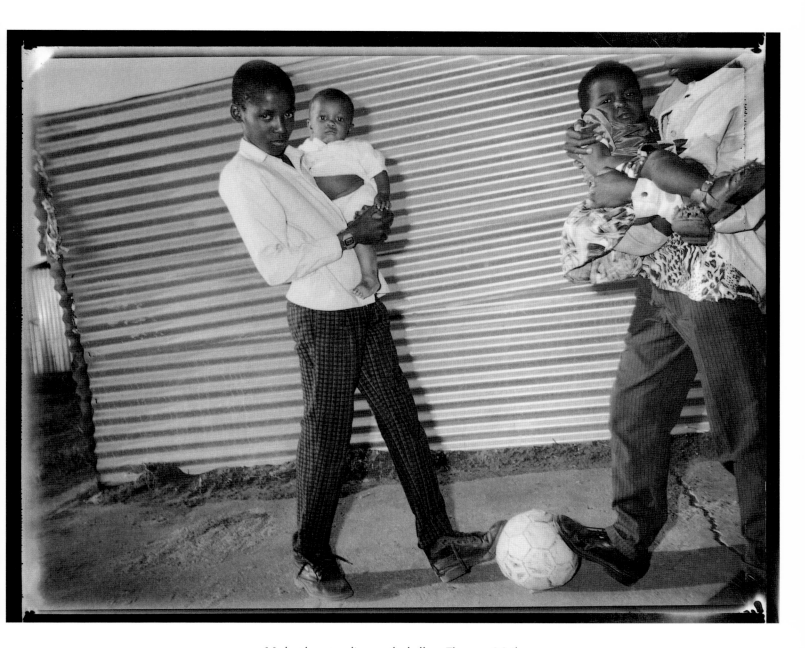

My brothers standing on the ball — Florence Maile

She is my sister sleeping on the table. — Victor Wotchela

The boys standing in the house playing — Bafana Radebe

Untitled — Rose Radebe

My parents are reading the Bible. — Robert Mbokane

My girl —Catharine Berry

My sister with a friend —Natasha Prinsloo

I am dead. — Palesa Molahloe

Untitled — René Jansen Van Vuuren

My brother with the guns — Catharine Berry

Granny having a smoke — Kaith Ntuli

My father and my brother's friend watching the television program,
"The Cow that Eats Alone" — Pamela Zungu

A group of the neighbor children standing in the street — René Jansen Van Vuuren

The men are dancing. — Florence Maile

My sister and her baby — Natasha Prinsloo

Untitled — René Jansen Van Vuuren

Neighbors in the yard —Anthony Kinnear

Morocco 1995

Asilah is a lovely port town seventy kilometers southwest of Tangiers. Matisse painted many of his vistas there, and lately it has been the home of an international arts festival. I lived and taught there, inside the *medina,* the walled city, next to the palace built by the pirate Rassouli in the 1800s. No cars could enter the *medina;* the only sounds were children playing in the narrow lanes, people chatting and arguing, and the waves crashing against the sea wall.

I came here to understand what the role of images — especially photographs — might be in the Muslim world. What part did text play? In India, surrounded by the intriguing characters of Hindi or Gujarati script, I had thought about the graphic potential of using words scratched onto the photographic negative, something akin to the carvings on the stone monuments of the village where I lived. I had asked a few of my students to scratch their names on portraits I'd made of them, but I was disappointed with the results. Now that I was in an Arabic-speaking country, where Koranic verses were commonly written in intricate patterns, it seemed appropriate to use words again. This time I allowed my collaborators to freely transform the portraits I made of them by drawing on the negative to the point of risking its destruction.

In Morocco my students were chosen from among the many schools inside and outside the city gates of Asilah. They were eager, but something about the aims they expressed for their pictures surprised me. Instead of planning to take pictures of childhood events, of their families or friends, they talked about making pictures that conserved their traditions. "I want to take pictures of plaster designs in the houses, monuments, mosques and embroidery," Fatima said. "Moroccan traditions get deep inside me because they make me remember my origins."

Though I anticipated some objections to making photographs of people in an Islamic country, I didn't realize what a challenge it would be for the children of Asilah to photograph their families and communities. The students kept reassuring me that it was alright, but when the girls returned with pictures they had taken, an unusually high percentage of the images were blurry.

At first they attributed it to the *sharki,* the strong, chill wind that blows off the Mediterranean. It was the *sharki,* they insisted, that jinxed the pictures. Either that, or one of the other girls had pushed the girl who was taking the picture. It took some time for them to get around to the real difficulties they had in taking pictures in the street. "People here have a complex," Rajae said. "They get a bad feeling when they see someone with a camera. They think they're preserving their traditions by not showing them to the rest of the world."

Amal, thirteen, and Khadija, fourteen, were my constant companions. About midway through the four months we spent together, they decided to observe the rules which require a woman to cover her body with a *jalaba,* a long shapeless robe, and her hair with a scarf. Given the relatively liberal atmosphere in Morocco their peers and even their parents thought this was odd, but it was their firm girlhood pact. It seemed to have begun the day they went to photograph the decorative patterns inside a *marabout,* a shrine where women often go to pray. There they encountered a girl possessed by a jinn, a spirit who had taken possession of the girl's body.

Portraits of Sakina Lafdaili, Ilias Benazzouz
Omar Arsalam, and Mohamed Boufelj

Portraits of Rajae Jabine, Hatar Breddadi,
Yassir Jbari, and Samira Chafik

Pigeons on the wall around the roof — Mohamed Karbab

They were talking about people. —Amal Malek

A picture of Mecca — Mohamed Bencharki

A sheep for Aid El Kabir —Sakina Lafdaili

Moroccan baker in a traditional oven — Yassir Jbari

My little sister is praying. — Mounia Betioui

The Jinn

Last night Amal and I were taking photos outside and we decided to go into the marabout, *the shrine of a particular saint, Sidi Alarghbi. We began to take photographs of the mosaics inside. Suddenly we saw a girl about fifteen or sixteen crying and shouting. We couldn't figure out what was happening. We tried to recite the Koran, but when we began, she screamed and we got scared. We stopped taking pictures because we were frightened that something might go wrong. We sat down with the girl. Her mother and little brother told us they were from Zinat, a neighborhood near Tangier. The girl's name was Zohra and a jinn was living inside her. The jinn of a Jew, God protect us, was living there.*

We wanted to go because we were frightened. The girl was shouting like a man; the jinn was making her do it. She had a hard, strong voice. It was saying, "I've been living inside her for a year and a half and I will not leave. I love her and I want to marry her."

"We will get rid of you by force," the girl's mother kept saying.

"Even if you take her all over the world to people who get rid of jinns, I will not leave. I'll kill her first."

"I have everything," the jinn continued, "I have weapons and gold. I have money. I have big buildings. I'll make sure you have everything you want. Just give me your daughter. I've always watched her smiling and laughing. Her hair is beautiful."

"I swear by God," the girl's brother said, "you're not going to take her. You're dreaming. You will never have my sister. You can kill me, but you can't have my sister."

"Look, I'm a very nice man," the jinn said. "I was only in her stomach — gurgling. If I did what I liked I could've made her disappear. I want to marry her in the right way, but the fkia, *the holy man in Ksar Kabir, discovered me and destroyed my plan."*

The brother asked Zohra to lay down and sleep on her mother's lap. The jinn said, "No, I'm not going to sleep on your mother's legs."

I told the brother he could recite the Koran and it would relax his sister. In the Koran God says, "I made the human and the jinn only to pray for me." The jinn heard me and yelled, "I'm not frightened by the Koran."

"You will be relaxed if you pray," I said to the girl. "Now we will leave you."

When we came back in the afternoon to ask about her, she and her brother were having a tough conversation. "You were shouting at me," the brother said. "You were insulting me."

"I'm sorry but I was not conscious of what was happening." She turned to us. "Excuse me if the same thing happened with you," and she knelt to pray.

It was very hard to distinguish between Zohra's voice and the jinn's. Sometimes when we thought she was talking, her voice was nearly a man's. Also she never went to school, so she knew only the Moroccan language, but the jinn spoke classical Arabic. "Ana Yahude," he said. "I am Jewish," in classical Arabic.

"I want to have the Koran," Zohra said to the jinn.

"I hate the Koran," said the jinn.

Now it was time for the fourth prayer. The girl said, "I want to go to pray because it makes me feel good afterwards. But maybe he will not let me go to pray. Brother, is it the fourth time to go to pray?"

"Yes."

"But he will not let me go to pray." She became furious. She started laughing strangely. We noticed she had bruises where we were told the jinn had hit her. She started to shout. Amal stepped backwards.

They took her to pray but she was wild and tried to escape. Her brother grabbed her.

"The jinn told me to escape with him to the beach," Zohra said. "He said he would let me pray on the beach."

A thirty-five-year-old woman came into the marabout to pray. When she started to leave, she lost control. She was shouting. She wanted to eat the people there but God protected us. "Look at that woman," the Jewish jinn yelled. "She has a Muslim jinn inside her. It was I who made the jinn furious." Then the Jewish jinn and the Muslim jinn shouted at each other like sheep bleating before the slaughter of the feast of Aid El Kebir.

Finally they put the woman in one of the chambers and chained her. She collapsed. After a while the Jewish jinn said to us, "Don't worry. I will speak with the jinn and he will be affectionate with the woman when she wakes up. She doesn't interest me. She has children and a husband, but I wanted to show you what I can do."

Then the Jewish jinn said to the Muslim jinn, "Leave that woman." After a while the woman woke up as if nothing had happened.

"You too," we said to the Jewish jinn. "You have to leave the girl and let her be free so she can marry a Muslim man."

"No. This I will never do. I love her. If you don't let me marry her, I'll kill her." He began to bang her head against the wall, but all you could see was her head hitting the wall.

"You must leave the girl," we said again.

"I won't. You know what it means to be a Jew. I must insist on what I want."

Her head kept banging against the wall.

"So what about me?" I said. "Do you think you could live inside me and leave the girl?"

"No way. I like her. I like her very much."

The girl's brother pushed the girl in the stomach. The jinn began to shout in a high voice, because he lives in the girl's stomach, "Let's go outside for a breath of air."

"No, I won't go outside with you if you don't leave my sister."

"Your sister is not yours. She's mine. I'm the one who guides her — not you or your mother."

The jinn spoke to the girl, "You prefer to marry an old man who has many children and has been married many times? I'm not married. I have a lot of planes and I will cover you with gold. I have everything you want. I can bring you dirhams from the deepest part of the sea.

"It was your cousin. She was jealous of you. She gave you a magic potion that brought me to you. Your cousin is your enemy." Only then did the family realize who was to blame.

The mother was crying. They chained the girl close to the wall because she'd been possessed when she went for water. She went to sleep and spent the night chained there. While she slept, the mother and another woman spoke in low voices. "You have to take her to Moulay Absalam," the woman said.

The jinn woke up. "Moulay Absalam! Even if you take her to all the holy men in the world, I'll never leave. Or I'll kill her."

*"I swear to you," Zohra's mother shouted, "you will not have my daughter."
Then the jinn said something to her softly over and over again. It was as if they were
bargaining.*

*"Now the girl belongs to me. You have to know that I'm Jewish. It's finished.
She's definitely mine. I have all of her. Maybe before it would have been different."*

*I told my mother this story and she gave me a beating. "If you go back there,
I'll cut your legs," she said. But we had to find out what had happened. The next
day there was no school, so we went to the* marabout *again.*

*When we entered we could hear the mother and the girl speaking. The girl
asked the mother to change her clothes for her. It was very difficult because the jinn
didn't want the mother to see the body of the girl.*

"I like Zohra when she's wearing nice clothes and looks pretty," the jinn said.

*The girl said to her brother, "Please give me a knife to cut the threads of this
dress." He was frightened she might kill herself, or the jinn might kill her because
he found it very hard to tell who was asking for the knife.*

*"No, don't worry," Zohra said. "I'm the one who is asking for the knife, not
the jinn."*

*They'd been to see the doctor earlier, the mother told us. "He said she had
a black liver that was half eaten. He thinks her sickness comes from the liver. Afterwards we went to the* fkia *and he's the one who told us that it was the jinn who
ate the liver. When I feed her she vomits even if it's light food. It's been a year and
a half that she's been vomiting."*

*The jinn told the mother, "You give her only water and bread. I'm giving
her paradise fruit, bananas and other fruits. I won't let her eat your food. What you
give her, I give it back to you."*

*The jinn sometimes says, "I've been living inside her for six years. I was
living in her many years ago. Then I left, but when I heard she was to be married
to the* haj *(old man) I came back."*

*We went back again yesterday. She was very normal. She was nice.
The jinn wasn't there. She was telling her brother that she knew the Jewish jinn was
inside her. She promised, "If the jinn leaves me, I will live with the* fkia *until the
next Aid El Kebir."*

"The fkia *told me that when she finishes hiccuping we can bring her to him,"* the mother said. *"Because if she's hiccupping it means the jinn is still inside her."*

She's still at the marabout. *We are friends with her now, but she's still hiccupping and she hiccups a lot. When the jinn wants to speak, he laughs before he talks. When the girl is normal, she's very tender.*

I'm afraid the jinn wouldn't let you try to record him. Even if the tape recorder is working, there will be no voice inside. We asked the fkia *about that. He said, "No, the jinn could never be recorded because he is hidden humanity and he knows every-thing even when he's sleeping." And you can't take a picture of him either. If we tried to take pictures there would be nothing. It would be black, I'm sure.*

— Khadija Breddadi with Amal Malek

A neighbor woman's sheep —Rabie Bencharki

He's scared he's going to be punished. — Yassir Jbari

My little sister, Hafsa — Rajae Jabine

The teapot is magically pouring tea in the glasses. — Abdsalam Namir

Untitled — Rabie Bencharki

The meat of the sheep — *Aid El Kabir* — Ilias Benazzouz

My sister in our garden fishing — Willeke van den Dool

The Netherlands 1996

When I received a commission from the Mondrian Foundation in Amsterdam to photograph the "changing Dutch identity," I hesitated, largely because of my experience in Morocco. My time there was rich in friendship and enlightenment, but the photographic work was a challenge almost impossible to overcome. Since Morocco had been a tourist destination for over a century, its people and landscape had been relentlessly documented. I was dubious about how the land of windmills and Hans Brinker and his Silver Skates would take to yet another image maker.

Still, I was fascinated by Holland's image as a quaint, homogeneously white European country and its new multi-cultural identity. In order to find out something about the image and reality of "being Dutch," I began to work in three very different communities.

Twice a week I held class for children at the Eben-Haezzer school, a Dutch Reformed school in the village of Ottoland. Ottoland is a small, close-knit farming community with conservative religious traditions.

My students at the Oscar Romero school in Rotterdam came from Morocco, Surinam, Cape Verde, the Dominican Republic, and what was formerly called Yugoslavia.

The third group had yet another culture, perhaps more stereotypically Dutch: they were nine- to thirteen-year-olds whose parents lived and worked on barges transporting goods along the waterways of The Netherlands, Germany and Belgium. During the school year these children lived at the Princess Irene boarding school in Schiebroek, a suburb of Rotterdam. It was quite an adjustment for them to live on land, with relatively limitless space. The school seemed so vast to one boy that he was unable to find the nearby bathroom. Another child had to learn how to walk up stairs.

The photographs taken by these three groups of children looked quite distinct, though all of them, it should be emphasized, dealt with space — with the way the landscape, the neighboring streets, or the interiors of ships were organized.

What the children from Ottoland did best of all, what they did most authentically, were precise renderings of landscapes and interiors. The immigrant children from the Oscar Romero school created lively, often chaotic compositions of people.

It occurred to me that the identity of the shippers' children might best be examined by photographing the rooms they decorated for themselves at the boarding school, and by inviting them to write on the negatives. Each room seemed designed to create the appearance of a normal childhood — though souvenirs of their peripatetic life pierced that illusion.

With all the children, I found that many of the images they made bore a striking resemblance — in choice of subject matter (often depopulated of human beings), in composition, and in their overriding sense of precision — to paintings and photographs from the past four centuries of Dutch art. Their photographs also seemed deeply meditative, and profoundly rooted in a landscape that is a culture in itself, a very specialized landscape reclaimed by twelve centuries of heroic ingenuity from the always-threatening sea that surrounds it.

The cows are walking to the barn. — Erika den Besten

My sister working on the computer — Willeke van den Dool

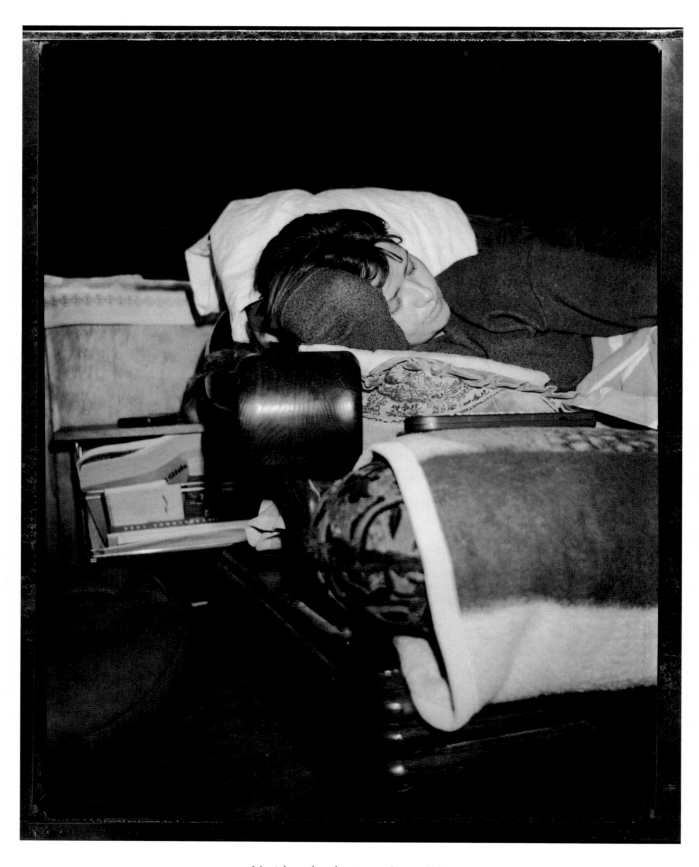

My sick mother sleeping — Soraya Beije

We are eating a nice meal, my father, my mother, Annemieke, and Bart. — Saskia de Jong

A white swan in the middle of the polder —Miranda Plooij

My brother's traveling store in front of the cheesemaker's house — Willeke van den Dool

Here my cousin is combing her hair. —Lucy Días Semedo

This is my cousin with some hot water. — Lucy Días Semedo

Jacob reading — Fatima el Farroudi

The thief caught in the living room — Fatima el Farroudi

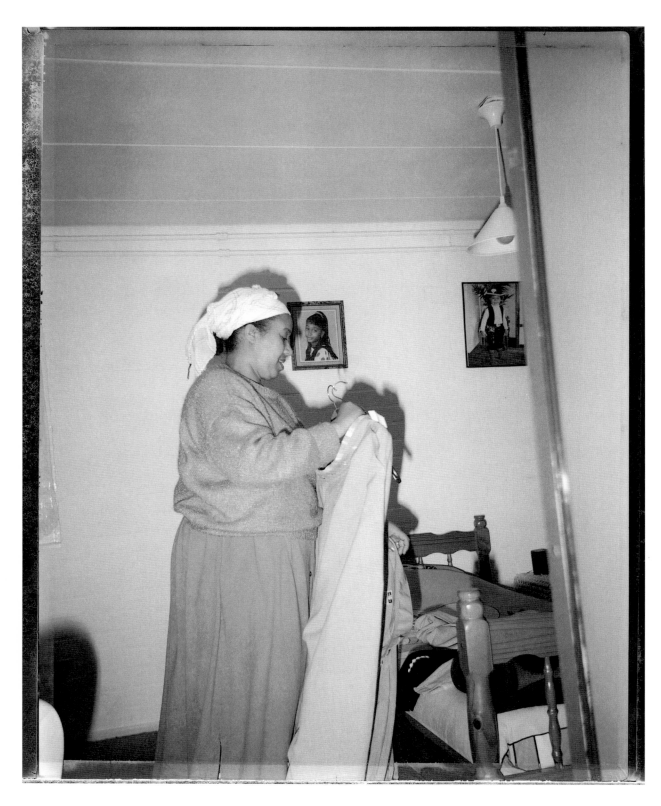

My mother in the bedroom — Fatima el Farroudi

Martijn is warming his hands over a little fire. — Frans Aantjes

The church in winter at five o'clock — Saskia de Jong

The polder behind my house — Dirk-Jan Aantjes

Gerdien Aanen

Lydia Bons

My name is Fatima and my birthday is in July.

Then I'll be 12. We now have Ramadan. I cannot do it sometimes, the fast. I like it when Wendy is here. We have a really nice time then. I don't like playing during the winter. It's too cold then. I've got two brothers and one sister. I am the biggest. I've got two more brothers. We have the same father, but not the same mother. The biggest brother is 21 and the other is 18. They are not married yet. They are very sweet. I am learning at home with my dad. My little brother goes to the mosque with my dad. He teaches the children Moroccan. My dad learned sixty stories from the Koran when he was little. My relatives live in Morocco. I went there by plane in July 1996. There I became ill. I got a rash from the heat. Then I got soap which made me better.

— Fatima el Farroudi

Michel's room

Erika den Besten

If I were pure white I wouldn't have friends.

If I were brown everybody would call me nigger.

If I were black everybody would call me shitboy.

If I were white I would just feel like that.

If I were red everybody would call me lighthouse.

If I were blue I would swim in the water.

If I were green I would lay in the tree.

If I were orange I would play for the Dutch football team.

If I were purple everybody would call me purple-head.

If I were yellow I would eat lots of lemons.

—Ahmed Hamdaoui

Daniel's room

Ronald's room

Saudi Arabia 1997

In Morocco I had begun to understand some of the subtleties of Islam and to experience its comforting effect on the town I was living in. Never before had I lived in a place that felt so safe; I imagined the *medina* as a womb surrounding me. But I still wanted to see what life might be like in a more strictly religious Islamic country. So far, as a Westerner, I had been able to avoid many of the restrictions placed on the people I worked with. To really understand such rules, I would have to live with and experience them personally.

Jeddah, on the west coast of the Kingdom of Saudi Arabia, is the port of entry for millions of pilgrims who travel to Mecca every year. The culture of the city is traditional, but perhaps because of its interaction with the entire Muslim world, it is open to new ideas. Still, photography is considered controversial; in much of the Muslim world, representational graphics can be construed as graven images. In Jeddah, people rarely take pictures in public, though many families do so at home. In addition to these considerations, there is a strict taboo against any mingling of the sexes and against public exposure of any part of a woman's body except for her hands and eyes.

Every morning and evening for two weeks, chauffeurs dropped off my students—professional women, housewives and schoolgirls—wrapped in *abayas* (shroud-like gowns) at the girls' school where my photography workshop was being held. (The women couldn't drive themselves because women are not allowed to drive in Saudi Arabia.) We decided that the most challenging subject we could explore was self-representation. I wanted to find ways in which the women could do this in a public arena. Many of the women chose to make pictures of themselves unveiled, photographs they knew could never be shown publicly. Others looked for metaphors to explain who they were, like Raja Alem, a writer, who used two shells to represent herself and her sister Shadia, a painter.

Finally I asked the women if they would work with me to make collaborative portraits that could be exhibited and published. After some discussion, it was agreed that they would need to cover themselves, or represent themselves in indirect ways.

Nadine chose her veiled daughter as her stand-in. At my suggestion she added her own hands. Anoud, because she was a young girl, was able to pose in Western clothes, without her *abaya*. Another young girl named Johainah chose a more traditional route: She pictured herself wearing her *abaya,* and holding her little sister. Later she asked if I would add more lines to the negative and further obscure her face.

Eventually an exhibition of these portraits, self-portraits, and dream pictures was mounted at Jeddah's House of Photography. The women decided that they wanted their work seen by an integrated audience; that is, by men and women. This meant that the images had to be carefully edited to get by the censors. Parts of some photographs had to be blocked out with Magic Markers to erase areas that revealed women's faces or bodies. Raja's portrait, which made use of an ancient Arabic text called *The Book of Dreams,* was culled by censors wary of controversial symbolism.

The exhibition opened with great fanfare. The opening night, which was for ladies only, was presided over by a princess of the Saudi royal family. The second night was for men only, and the third was for husbands and wives together.

Sleeping with my shoes —Al Sharifa Noha AlGhalib

Crying for my face —Al Sharifa Noha AlGhalib

Nadine holding her daughter

Who am I? 1970–1997 — Nadine Faisal Binzagler

All Kinds of Veils

High in the mountains of Saudi Arabia, carved and painted on cliffs, there are many prehistoric pictures of horses and human beings. Since the beginning of time, these images have had no respite from prying idolizing eyes. For those of us who live in a culture as ancient as Saudi Arabia's, the historical and spiritual weight of these images suggests that making portraits is no light matter. Taking someone's photograph is equivalent to capturing his twin self, his spirit; it is a way of taking complete control of the person whose picture is taken. Photography is a glimpse into the soul, stolen for the sake of illuminating a dark, impersonal sheet of paper.

In this case photography turned out to be something more. It began when we allowed an outsider to see behind the veil. Then, assuming the role of hunters put us in another realm and gave us a place to stand that was powerful enough to alter the male-controlled orbits we move in. When we took our cameras into the street, people reacted with sincerity and entertained new possibilities. The bodies they had lived in so long opened to whatever experiences they might encounter. They seemed oblivious to the dangers of intrusion or captivity. They opened up and posed happily, smiling at the camera's charm and at our courage in openly pursuing stories in circumstances that are ordinarily closed. By posing, they allowed us to steal their souls. And in the very act of announcing our power, we women gained power over the men.

—Raja Alem

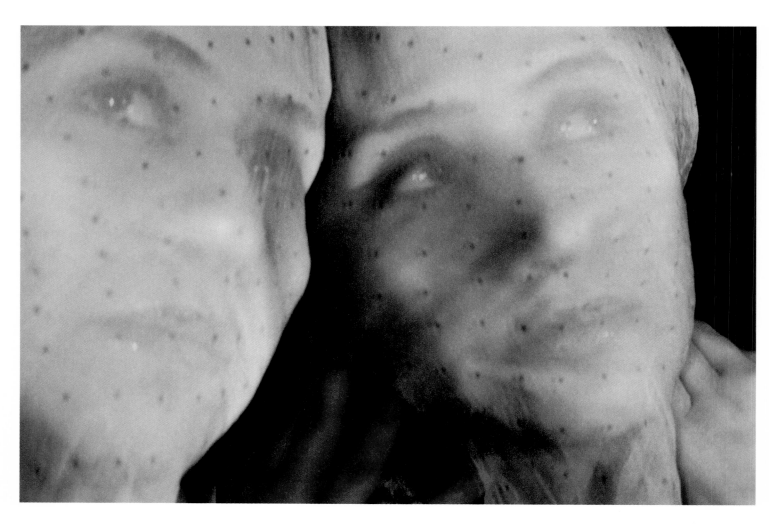

Self-portrait — Raja Alem

Self-portrait — Raja Alem

Twin sisters #1 — Raja Alem

The Queen of all queens in the kingdom of keys. . . .
Each key controls thousands and thousands of spirits,
And each spirit has thousands of followers.
Each spirit rules thousands and thousands of giants.
This is written in ink made of alum.

I own the keys of creation.
This is written in ink made of alum.

Foreheads and fingers are merely doors to the invisible world.

The letter A is the king of the alphabet,
But it is silenced by Ibn Sereen's Book of Dreams.

— Raja Alem (translation of inscription on photograph)

Shadia Alem

Johainah holding her little sister

Johainah's portrait —Versace on the holy basil plant

Michael and my cousin in our front yard. Don't be ashamed to show your face. —Tiffany Best

Durham 1989–1999

My life abroad was so stimulating and transforming that I often felt a complete stranger when I returned to the United States. The constant moving from project to project and place to place left me feeling homeless, and being out of the country made it difficult to raise the money I needed to continue working. It seemed clear that I needed a base from which to work and a group of people who would share my enthusiasm for the work I was doing.

So in 1989, when I was asked by the Center for Documentary Studies at Duke University to conduct a workshop in two elementary schools, I used it as an opportunity to create a photography and writing program directed toward the public schools in Durham, North Carolina. I wanted to build a program that would influence an entire school system and would serve as a laboratory for my own work. I would try out my ideas about collaborative image-making and share them with classroom teachers who might find them useful. (Currently fourteen elementary and middle schools participate in what we call "Literacy Through Photography.")

I started with three schools. Teachers selected students according to their artistic potential and need for extra stimulation in the classroom. In one case, the child of a mixed marriage was included to help her articulate the problems of her unusual background in an all-black school.

Many of the students lived in communities where violence was common. It came as a surprise to them to be given responsibility for using and looking after the cameras, and making photographs in the darkroom. At first it was difficult for many of them, particularly the more troubled kids, to concentrate on making pictures. Cameras were opened in mid-role, ruining pictures already taken, film was lost.

A fourth-grade student named Phillip was said to have the highest IQ in the school. His intelligence and creativity were evident in the few comments he made in class, but he could not concentrate, and often he misplaced or ruined his film. Though he never wanted to leave photography class, he never really got anything accomplished. One day I encouraged him to write a rap poem. It was the first task he was able to finish. He continued to write short pieces with powerful lines —"I have a jungle right beside my house. My community is like a drug bust"— and soon he found his misplaced rolls of film. As I suspected they would be, the photographs turned out to be beautiful, strangely composed glimpses into Phillip's mind.

In time I came to know the Durham community through my students. I began to trust my ability to ask meaningful questions. How did they feel, for example, about race, religion, about their own identities?

Since the teachers themselves had started teaching photography and writing to their students, I was free to create new projects based on these questions. The mid-sized racially and ethnically mixed city of Durham became fertile ground on which I could create models that could be used in other culturally divided environments.

I am alone in the wilderness —Phillip Liverpool

My sister and her cousin have a job at doll beauty world —Lateisha Harris

From left to right: *Izak; I'm going to fall* —Phillip Liverpool; *Untitled* —Lateisha Harris; *Untitled* —Lateisha Harris;
A still life with a picture of me —Kelly Mitchell; *Now what key is it? My mom, Aminah* —Maryam Nubee;
My aunt and uncle, they're married. I told them I wanted a romantic moment, so they gave it to me —Tiffany Best

Mister Frazier and Mrs. Abbot, one of the t-ball photographers —Najma Marks

MmMm — Drew is eating a hot dog —Phillip Liverpool

Untitled —Nicole Hargrave

My community in the city —Lateisha Harris

Jungle Music III: Drew and Taylor —Phillip Liverpool

The Alphabet Project 1997

For many years North Carolina has been a stop on the Central America –
Texas – Carolina migrant stream. Workers follow the tobacco and
vegetable harvests, sometimes far into the northeastern states, before
returning home. Some of the migrants have "settled out;" they have
taken up permanent residence in the United States. Many of them
don't speak English, and many are not citizens.

During my years in Latin America, I came to appreciate the
sophistication of the language and the cultures I was working in. It was
disheartening, therefore, to hear stories from the English-as-a-Second-
Language teachers in Durham about the bad treatment their students
sometimes received from other teachers, who assumed, because the children didn't speak English, that they were stupid.

When I adopted a baby boy from Latin America, I became even
more sensitive to the situation of Latino children in the American schools.
How would my own son be treated, even though he spoke English?
I began to think about ways in which photographs could be used to teach
language. As a first step I decided to create an alphabet with Spanish-
speaking children in grades two through five, for whom English was a
second language. First we discussed the concept of language and where
in the world different languages were spoken. I asked the students
to think of words in their own language beginning with each letter of
the alphabet, and to assign them visual representations from their
culture. I photographed each concept or object they selected. When the
negatives were ready, the children scratched them or wrote on them with
Magic Markers, adding the letter and word they were illustrating on the
white or black background. They talked about how English-speaking
children were mistrustful of them when they spoke Spanish. They were
happy to be working on a project in their own language, a project they
could share with others. I found the words they used — like *nervioso* or
impostor — to be revealing about the often transitory nature of their lives.

Photographs with
Isai Delgado,
Omero Cruz,
Francisco Melo,
Francisco Bautista,
Zulio Garcia,
Jorge Canuto,
Victor Mendez,
Edgar Hernández,
Andreina Delgado,
Kevin Colindres,
Jennifer Lizama,
Janette Alarcón,
Carlitos Canuto,
and Edgar Orozco

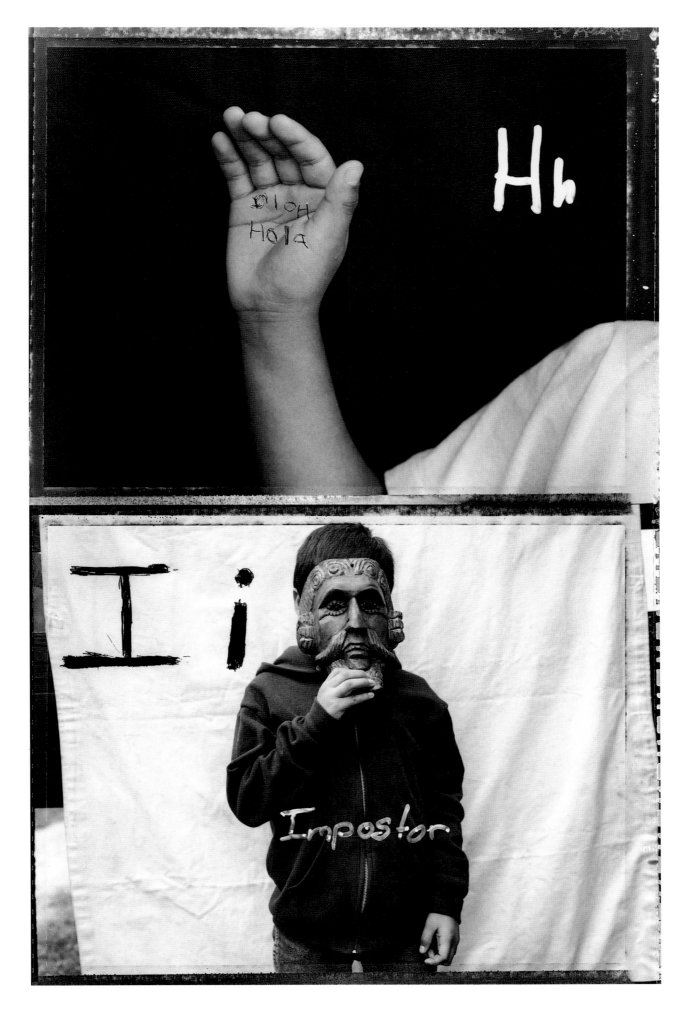

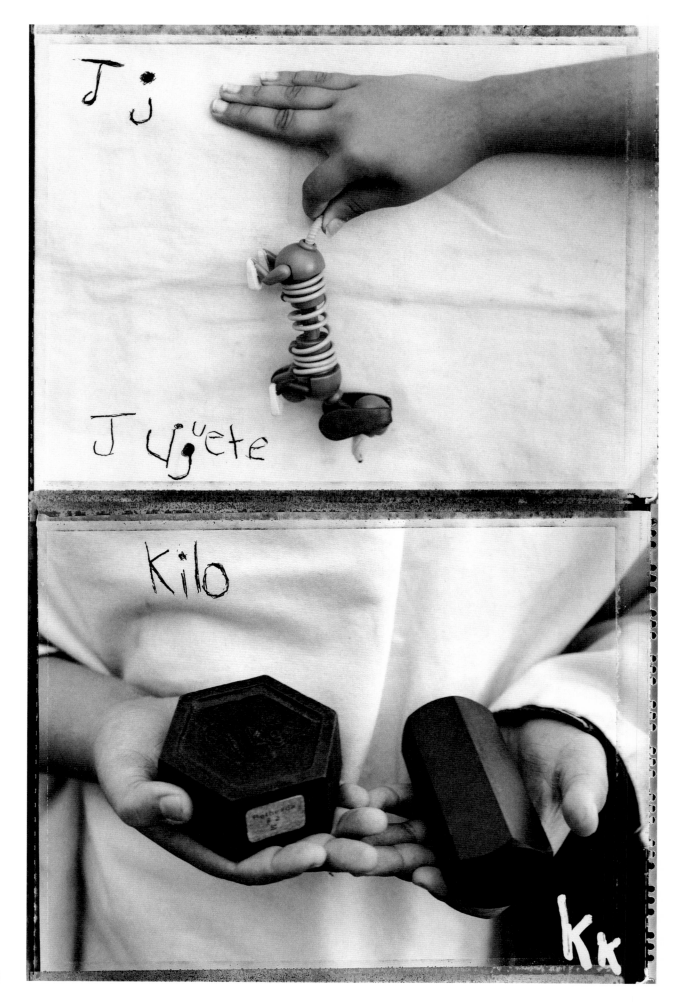

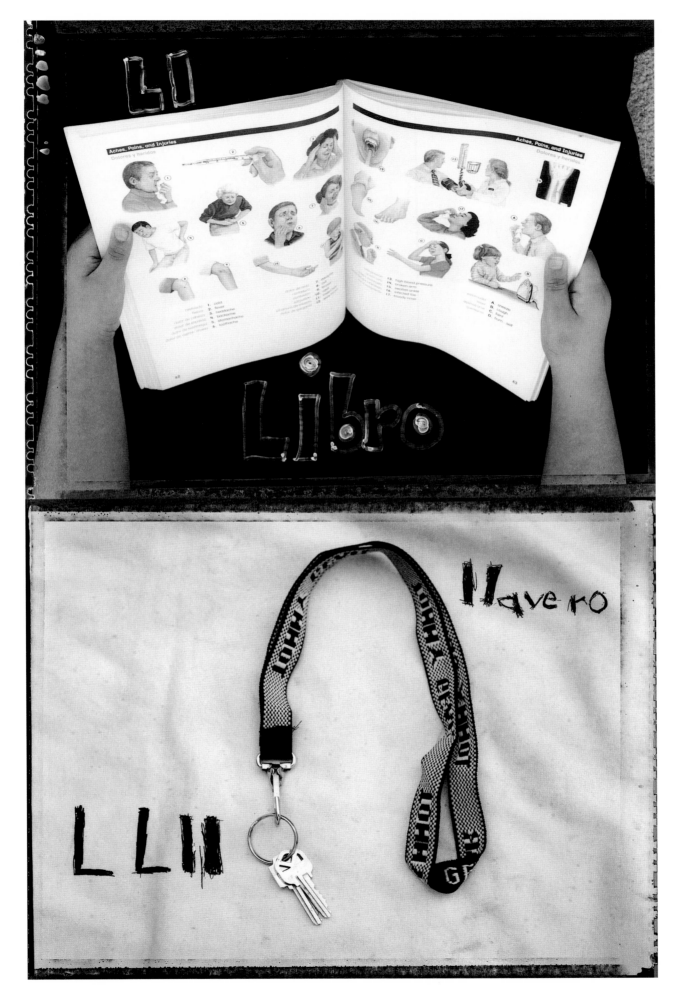

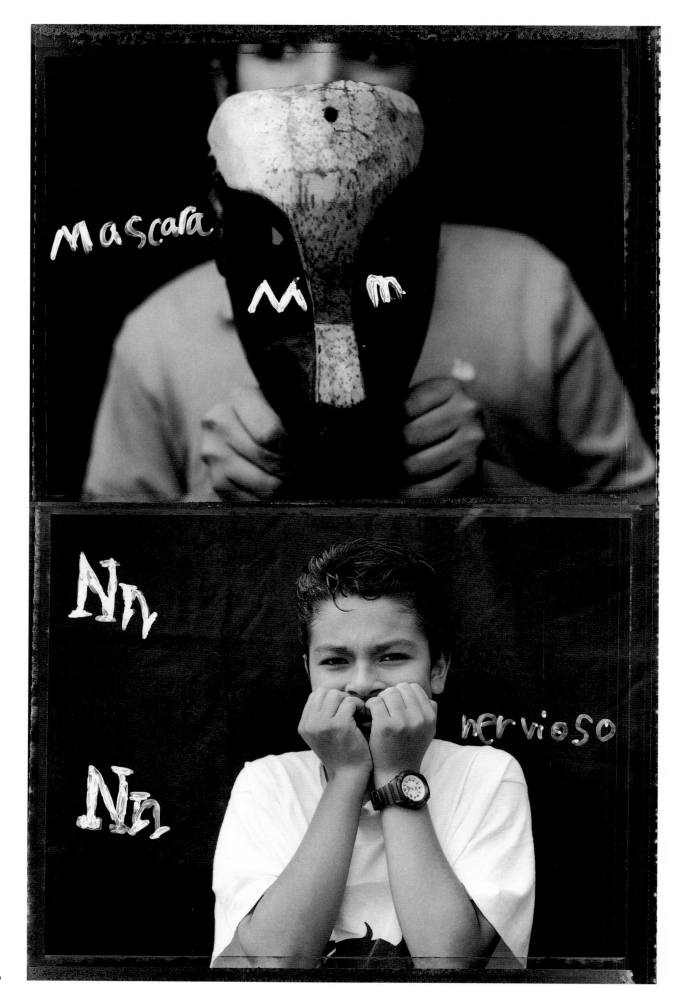

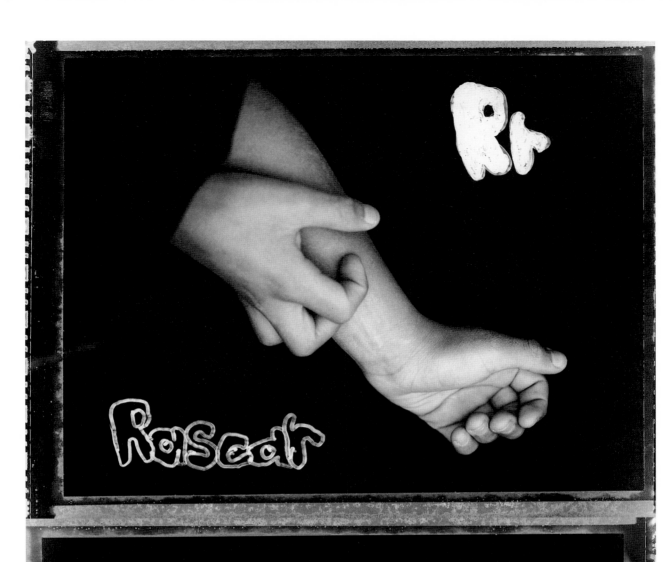

Rr

Rascar

rr

Is a single letter in the spanish alphabet.

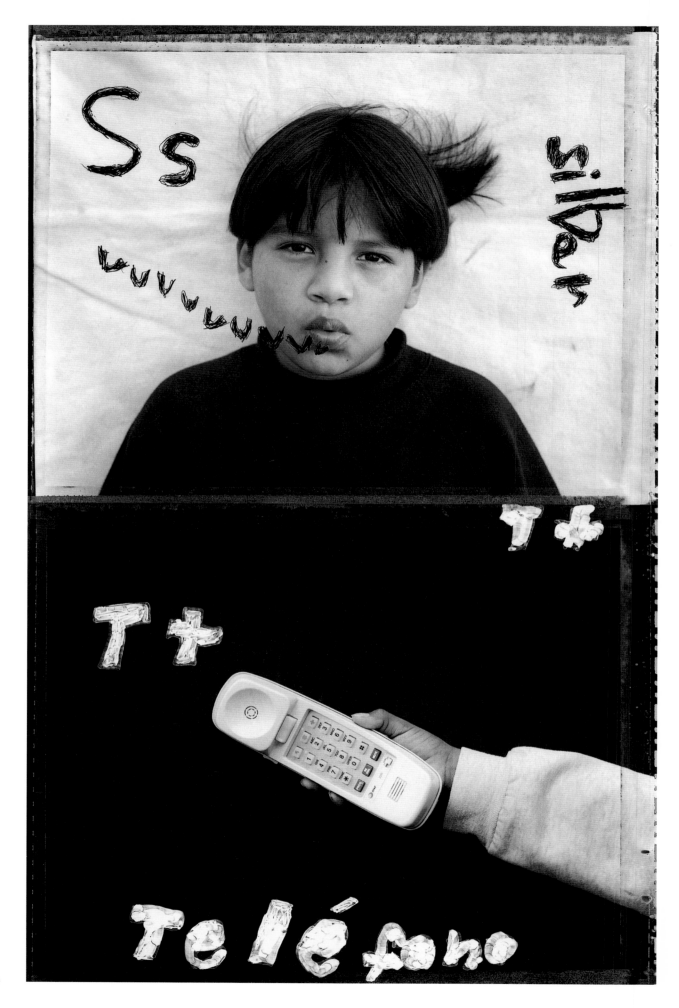

Ww

letter not belonging to the Spanish alphabet and found only in foreign words.

Black Self/White Self 1994–1997

When I began working in Durham's inner city, I knew that I was being looked at as a white lady from a powerful white university. I was reminded of my days in Detroit during the 1960s; I had decided then that it was time for whites to step aside from the "Black Power" struggle. It was twenty years later now, and I hadn't worked in an African American community since then.

Over the past two decades, as more and more of Durham's white population moved to the suburbs, the public schools became segregated along city–county lines. Proposals to merge the school systems were stymied by objections from both sides. The African American children I worked with had never attended school with whites; many said they preferred it that way.

In 1992 the Durham school systems were finally merged. In 1994 I designed a collaborative project that looked directly at the issue of race. I asked children to write about themselves, then to write another version, this time imagining themselves as members of another race. This assignment was greeted first with silence, then laughter, and finally with an enthusiastic barrage of questions: Could they change their names as well as their race? Their families? How could they know what it was like to be of a different race?

It was difficult for some of the students to visualize themselves as "the other." Since the white children rarely dealt with the black world's perceptions of them, they had almost no idea of how to pose; some of them asked the African American children to direct them. The African American children never needed coaching: without saying a word, Antonio Gunther slumped over in front of a white seamless background and covered his head to represent what he explained was his white persona — homeless, without a community.

The African American children had a clearly defined sense of how they were seen by white people. Sometimes they internalized this image, as when they talked about their white selves being "nicer or smarter." As for the white children, they seemed almost naively optimistic. Chris Stollings, a white fifth-grader, said he imagined himself as the first black president.

Once the children had completed their written portraits, I photographed them posing as their "black" and "white" selves, using props they had brought from home. I gave them the large-format negatives to alter or write on, in keeping with ideas from their written portraits, so they could further describe the characters they had imagined themselves to be.

Because we were working with negatives, which reverse the polarity of black and white in the world as it is usually seen, they had to think carefully about scratching the emulsion in order to produce a black line, or adding a black mark to make a white line. In this way, negative and positive, and black and white, took on a meaning both conceptual and material.

I am a celebrity. I live in a mansion. I can beat anybody, even Bruce Lee, Chuck Norris, Steven Segal. I love school. My favorite subjects are gym, spelling, reading and language. I will be glad to get out of fifth grade and pass all my grades. I'm not boring like my friends.

My favorite music is rap, country and rock and roll. My hair is blond. My eyes are greenish. I'm pale skinned. I'm a muscleman. My favorite shoe is Reebok. My favorite sports are gymnastics, basketball, football, and hockey. My mother's name is Sara Jane. My brothers' names are Kendall, DJ, Mack, and Gregory.

Black Self/White Self with Leah Ceprano, Myricale Jacobs,
Brandy Bishop, Brandon Clark, Zavier Vereen, Jesse Beck, Jordan Daniel, Michael Green,
Douglas Bennett, Heather Rose, Anthony Burdick, Antonio Gunter, Gregory Blake,
Yashica Chioma Johnson, Chris Stollings, Courtney Hayes, and Chris Shepard

294

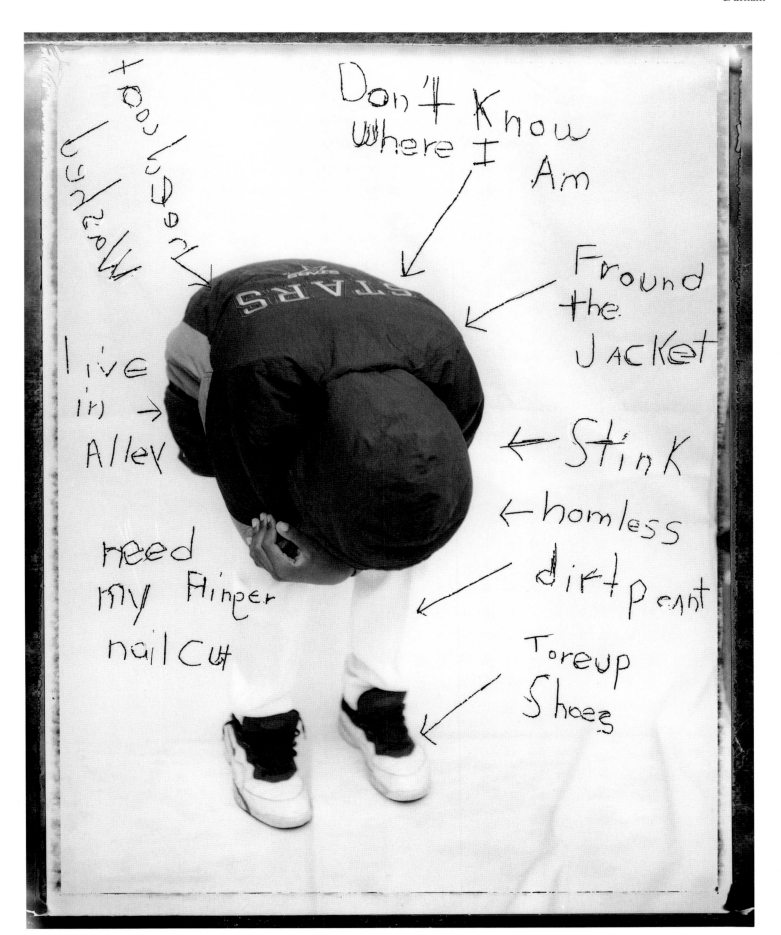

My name is Jonathan Tarp. I live in Washington, D.C. I want to be the first black president. I think I can be because I'm nice, fair, and have good judgement and if I can't be president, I'll be a cartoonist. My favorite food is pizza. My favorite color is blue. I'm a nice person. I love pets. I have two albino mice, Pinky and Brain, a calico kitten, Coco, and two dogs. Their names are Sparkey and Shadow. I can draw well. I have blue-green eyes, brown hair. I'm about five foot. I have a nice school for college. I want to go to Harvard.

My name is Natasha. I listen to rap. My favorite rap group is Queen Latifa.
My favorite music group is Boyz II Men and 69 Boyz. My hair is wavy and black.
My favorite month is December. My best friend has the smallest nose in the world.
My favorite state is New Jersey. My favorite color is blue. My favorite movie is
Boyz in the Hood. *I wear Filas. My best friend lives in Springfield Apartments.*
She has three sisters. We like to go to the movies and to do our homework in
the library. I have brown eyes and am very tall. I'm wearing a Walkman, vans,
coat, jeans and a Woodstock shirt.

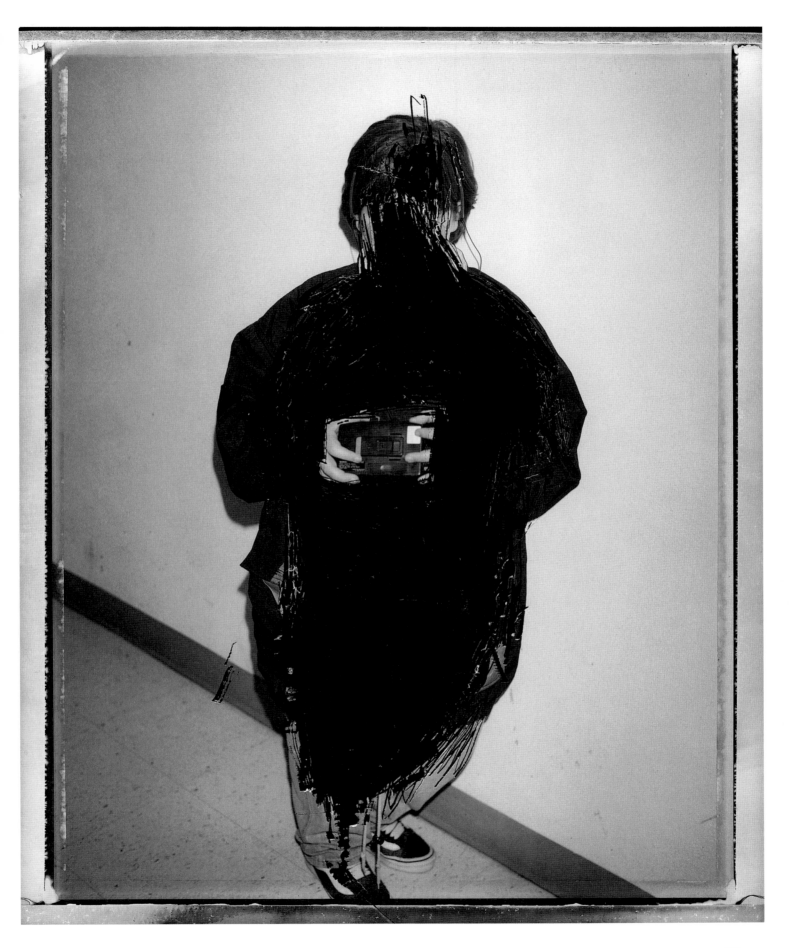

white
self

I like to draw, watch TV. I like to watch Garfield and Power Rangers. I love to play
basketball and baseball. I like to read Garfield comics. My favorite subject is spelling.
My favorite color is green. My favorite movie is The Mask *and* Street Fighter.
I have blond hair and blue eyes. My favorite team is the Forty-Niners. I love, love,
love, love UNC (University of North Carolina), and I love myself more than anything,
even more than UNC, my favorite.

I like rap. My favorite rap music is Boyz II Men. I like to eat seafood. I like to play basketball. I like to play video games. I am eleven years old. My favorite color is hot pink. I have glasses. My favorite team is the Chicago Bulls. My favorite state is New Jersey.

If I was white, 1) I will change my name to Jonathan on Family Matters.

2) People will call me a Saltine. 3) I will be a rock star on stage. 4) I will stay in school.

5) Going to funerals will be different. 6) I would like going to Greek restaurants.

I am 1) Silly 2) Have dark brown hair. 3) I'm scared of snakes. 4) I like dancing and singing. 5) I like to swim. 6) I like track and field. 7) I like to talk on the phone. 8) I like to play with my dog. 9) My favorite team is North Carolina. 10) My favorite food is pizza.

314

If I were black, I would have black skin and black hair. My name would be Karina. I would have brown eyes and kind of long hair. I would also be scared of my brother because he would always tease me and I don't like that. I would feel excited when I play hand games, when I do my crafts, when I jump rope or when I play with my other friends. I would like basketball, soccer, dancing and a lot of other sports. I would like shows like Martin, Roc, Boy Meets World and Home Improvement.

I would do my homework every afternoon so I would have it done at night. I would do that so I could watch those shows. In the classroom I would get most of it done. My friends and I would always play on the school playgrounds. It is really fun. I especially would like the twisty bar. It is the most fun of all.

I have green eyes, blond hair, white skin, and I wear neat clothes. I have five people in my family. I have four pets. They are a dog and three hermit crabs. I get mad at my brother because he wants to make my room into an arcade.

I love stuffed animals, especially my teddy bear. He is a panda bear. His name is Greypes. He is grey and white. He is so cute. I like taking lunch out on the picnic table. I take Greypes. He doesn't eat, so I eat it for him. I also love to take pictures and look at them. Greypes likes to look at them, too. We look at them on the playground.

Conclusion

Whenever I ventured out in the world as a child, I felt there was a bubble surrounding me, a bubble of privilege which kept me from interacting with the world. The bubble, I imagined, was made of tough, clear plastic that muffled all sound. For many years after I left home, the bubble would return when I was walking down a busy street in the company of my parents. With the bubble around us, no one could touch us.

The projects presented here led me on an odyssey out of that frightening comfort zone. The journey continues. My work has evolved as a description of my interaction with the world around me.

When I first started making photographs, I was fascinated by documentary efforts to catalogue social and economic problems of the 1930s and the occasional successes of social reforms. I was drawn to the use of photographs to influence legislation. As I came of age in the 1970s, when access to images from virtually all parts of the world became commonplace, I wondered what useful role photography might play. In addition to these social concerns, I had been schooled in photography as an art form, and this led me to keep esthetic considerations in mind.

When I first began to teach with photography, I regarded my pictures as separate from my students' work. I used my teaching skills to help them create the photographs I sensed they were capable of making. Gradually I realized that I was working much like a choreographer with dancers or a director with actors. My job was to recognize the uniqueness of each child's vision and nurture this vision to produce photographs. I kept in mind what Merce Cunningham once described as the basis for his choreography: "Each person has his own way of walking."

I was conscious, too, of the educational value of my work. I could see the children gaining self-confidence as they became fluent in a new medium. They often made discoveries about themselves while examining their surroundings. And sometimes the students' photographs of their home life helped their teachers understand them better.

My solo work had a different bent. When Luveena Holcomb, one of my neighbors in Kentucky, watched me moving back and forth to compose a picture of her gazing out the window of her house, she remarked that I was like "an old hen trying to make her nest." It was true — I fussed around a bit when I began making portraits. I wanted to make a different kind of documentary photography, one that called for the subject to create an enactment for my large-format camera of some event I had seen them involved in or a scene I imagined from stories I had heard them tell.

For some time I worked with two methods — solo and collaborative — that ran parallel, as it were, until I came to understand that it was possible to combine them. Whether I was teaching or photographing, the crucial part of my artistic process was human interaction. What was it, finally, that I was doing? Was it some kind of visual anthropology? Was it education? Photography? Could I combine these elements and be an artist too? Was there something less artistic about my work as a teacher than as a photographer?

With time I learned to back off from the world and let it reveal itself to me, and as I did, my projects became more conceptual. Each project became a distinct challenge to see beneath surface relationships. In response to each new subject, I tried to shift the vantage point by using new approaches and different materials. As the work progressed and I became more conscious of my method, I was able to experiment with ways of sharing control over the image-making.

Photography as the discipline I was schooled in came to feel stylistically predictable. Yet it continued to fascinate me as a medium in itself because in order to make photographs, you have to be there with your subject. The active dialogue between the photographer and the subject (and inevitably the viewer) became for me the essential point of a photograph. Beyond esthetic choices, I came to see photography as a language to which everyone has access. I began to feel closer to those pictures on the walls of the library in my parents' house. The more I could sense the presence of the person behind the camera, the more compelling these quite ordinary pictures seemed.

When my grandfather founded his advertising agency during the early days of mass production, he put images in the service of marketing. He was one of the people who created commercial photography and in doing so he had a lot to do with limiting the ways in which images are read. I often feel as if I'm destined to undo his work.

Teaching for me is a political act — if politics addresses the power or powerlessness of people in their everyday lives. I want people to understand the powers that use them and the powers they use — whether it be the power of a government or a parent or a religion. Sometimes I think I disguise myself as a teacher in order to make the pictures I need to see.

Wendy Ewald

1951   Born in Detroit, Michigan

1969 – 74   Attended Antioch College, Yellow Springs, Ohio. Studied photography
with Minor White.

1969 – 73   Photographed and taught Naskapi and MicMac children in Labrador
and New Brunswick, Canada.

1975 – 81   Founded and ran the Mountain Photography Workshop at Appalshop,
Whitesburg, Kentucky. Directed and participated in National Endowment for
the Arts photographic survey project. Edited and contributed to *Appalachia:
A Self Portrait,* a book of photographic essays created for the project. Taught
photography in three rural elementary schools as part of the Artist-in-the-Schools
program. Curated an exhibition of students' photographs for the Smithsonian
Institute, Washington, D.C. Published *Portraits and Dreams: Photographs and
Stories by Children of the Appalachians.*

1982 – 86   Won a Fulbright fellowship to photograph and teach in Colombia.
An exhibition of the work, "Retrato de un Pueblo", shown at the Museo de Arte
Moderno in Bogotá. Published *Magic Eyes: Scenes from an Andean Girlhood,*
a collaborative book of stories and photographs.

1988 – 89   Photographed and taught in India. Students' photographs exhibited in
Bombay at the Center for Photography as an Art Form and at Fotofest, Houston,
Texas. Received a National Endowment for the Arts Fellowship.

1991   Taught photography in Chiapas, Mexico. "Retratos y Suenos: Photographs by
Mayan and Mexican Children" shown at the George Eastman House, Rochester,
the Ansel Adams Center, San Francisco, the Center for Creative Photography,
Tucson, Arizona, and the Southeast Museum of Photography, Daytona Beach,
Florida.

1991 – 94   Became a senior research associate at Duke University's Center for
Documentary Studies. Started the "Literacy through Photography" program
for Durham Public Schools, North Carolina. Began working on a portrait
series with students in North Carolina.

1992 Worked with South African children in Orange Farm, a squatters' settlement, Glenesk, an Afrikaner neighborhood, and Soweto. Received a MacArthur Fellowship.

1994 Began "Black Self/White Self," the first in a series of collaborative projects with students and teachers in the Durham Public Schools.

1995 Went to Asilah, Morocco, to work with young artists and children at the Centre Hassan II. Published first in a series of photographic essays in *Doubletake* magazine.

1996 *I Dreamed I Had a Girl in My Pocket,* a book of stories and photographs from work in India, was published by W.W. Norton. Received a commission from the Mondrian Foundation in Amsterdam to create a project on Dutch identity.

1997 Traveled to Qatar and Saudi Arabia to hold photography workshops for men, women, and girls. An exhibition of the work was held in Jeddah. Participated in the 1997 Whitney Biennial. Received a commission from the Ackland Museum at the University of North Carolina to create an exhibition with children from five faith communities. Dutch work published in *Constructing Identities/ Photoworks in Progress.*

1998 Became research scholar at the Center for International Studies and the Program in Education at Duke University. Commissioned by the American Joint Jewish Distribution Committee to create a piece for the exhibition "To The Rescue: Eight Artists in an Archive;" worked with students in Durham to create a video installation. Visiting Fellow at the Townsend Center for Humanities at the University of California. Exhibition of large prints at the University of California at Berkeley Art Museum and Pacific Film Archive.

1999 "To The Rescue: Eight Artists in an Archive" shown at the International Center of Photography, New York City, and the Miami Art Museum. "Visions of Faith: Photographs by Wendy Ewald and Children" exhibited at the Ackland Art Museum, Chapel Hill, North Carolina.

2000 "Secret Games: Wendy Ewald, Collaborative Works 1969–1999" shown at Fotomuseum in Winterthur, Switzerland. Publication of *Secret Games: Wendy Ewald, Collaborative Works with Children 1969–1999* by Scalo Zurich–Berlin–New York.

2001 *The Best Part of Me,* a book on the body made in collaboration with Durham
students, published by Little, Brown and Co. "Secret Games" exhibited at
Addison Gallery of American Art, Andover, Massachusetts.

Bibliography

Appalachia: A Self-Portrait, edited by Wendy Ewald. Gnomon Press,
Kentucky, 1979.

Portraits and Dreams: Photographs and Stories by Children of the Appalachians.
Writers and Readers, New York and London, 1985.

Appalachian Women: Three Generations. Appalshop, Whitesburg,
Kentucky, 1981.

Retrato de un Pueblo. El Museo del Arte Moderno, Bogotá, 1982.

Magic Eyes: Scenes from an Andean Girlhood. Bay Press, Seattle, 1992.

I Dreamed I Had a Girl in My Pocket. W.W. Norton, New York, 1996.

Photowork(s) in Progress/Constructing Identity, edited by Linda Roodenburg.
Snoeck-Ducaju and Zoon, Gent, 1997.

To the Rescue: Eight Artists in an Archive. American Joint Jewish Distribution
Committee, New York City, 1999.

Visions of Faith: Photographs by Wendy Ewald and Children.
Ackland Art Museum, Chapel Hill, North Carolina, 1999.

Secret Games: Wendy Ewald, Collaborative Works with Children 1969–1999.
Scalo, Zurich, Berlin, New York, 2000.

The Best Part of Me. Little Brown and Co., Boston, New York, Toronto,
London, 2001.

I Wanna Take Me a Picture: Teaching Photography and Writing to Children.
Beacon Press, Boston, 2001.

Acknowledgments

For Tom and Michael and all my other collaborators

I must thank my immediate family for supporting me in what looked at times like a misguided adventure. I would especially like to thank my mother, Carolyn Ewald Kratzet, my late father Ted Ewald, and my sister Holly Ewald. My British cousins, Adrian and Michael Gill and Yvonne Gilan, first exposed me to another culture and to the world of artists.

For my work in Canada so many years ago I am indebted to the Quebec Labrador Mission Foundation, which continues to work with children and the environment. Thanks also to Appalshop, the multi-media cooperative that records the life and culture of Appalachia. My project in India was aided by the Self-Employed Women's Association, a union of home-based workers. For my work in Mexico I owe thanks to Sna Jtz-ibajom, a Mayan writers' cooperative, and to Pequeño Sol and Cuxtitali schools. In South Africa I received help from the Market Photography Workshop, and in Morocco I was helped by the Centre Hassan II, a cultural institute that encourages young artists. In The Netherlands I received support from the Nederlands Foto Instituut, and the Oscar Romero, Eben-Haezzer and Princess Irene schools. My work in Saudi Arabia was conducted under the auspices of the House of Photography in Jeddah.

In all these places, of course, there were individuals who extended their special help. I think of Elizabeth Barrett and Dee Davis at Appalshop, Ezequiel Alarcón, Carlos Mejía, Adelaida Trujillo, and John Orbell in Colombia, Renana Jhabvala, Darhshana Dalvi and Jyoti Jumani in India; Barry Norris, Antonio Turok, Francisco Xilón and Antonio de la Torre in Mexico; Victor Matom, Santu Mofekeng, Johnny Onverwacht, T.J. Lemon and David Goldblatt in South Africa; Souhail Benazzouz, Otman El Kasbi and Mohamed Benaissa in Morocco; Linda Roodenburg, Jan Vink and Herma Verweg in The Netherlands, and Lora Berg and Raja and Shadia Alem in Saudi Arabia.

Funding and materials for the projects came from many sources, among them: the Polaroid Corporation and Foundation, the Kentucky Arts Commission, the Fulbright Commission, the Educational Foundation of America, Kodak Worldwide, the Ricoh Corporation, the Lila Wallace Reader's Digest Fund, the National Endowment for the Arts, the Mondrian Foundation, the United States Information Service, and the Lyndhurst and MacArthur Foundations, who awarded me fellowships that gave me time to do much of this work.

I am deeply grateful to the Center for Documentary Studies and the Center for International Studies at Duke University and to the Durham Public Schools for providing a home for me these past ten years. It was Iris Tillman Hill at the Center for Documentary Studies and Alan Teasley of the Durham Public Schools who first saw the potential of my program in Durham; they continue to fight for it. School principals Audrey Boykin, Carolyn Rideout and Queen Bass have also stuck with me. I have had the privilege of working with many fine teachers, especially Emelia de la Croix, Kathy Fine, Robert Hunter, and Lisa Lord.

The staff at the Center for Documentary Studies at Duke University has helped me carry out many projects. I want to thank Alex Harris, Alex Lightfoot, Marta Urquilla, Ann Thomas, Dave DeVito, Dominique Phillips, Julia Hoggson, Dwayne Dixon and Katie Hyde — and Rob Sikorski at the Center for International Studies.

For "Literacy Through Photography," which is a project of the Center for Documentary Studies, we received grants from the Andy Warhol Foundation, the Nathan Cummings Foundation, the National Endowment for the Arts, the North Carolina Arts Council, the Surdna Foundation, the General Electric Foundation, the Open Society, and the Triangle Community Foundation for the Qualex Fund.

For the opportunity to create the exhibition which accompanies this book I should thank Jock Reynolds at the Addison Gallery of American Art and Alex Harris and Iris Tillman Hill at the Center for Documentary Studies. My friend and mentor Adam D. Weinberg and Allison Kemmerer of the Addison Gallery, Andover, Massachusetts, as well as Urs Stahel at the Fotomuseum in Winterthur, Switzerland, helped me give structure to thousands of images and hundreds of pages of text. Bill Anton contributed a sensitive and elegant design.

Pete Mauney has worked side-by-side with me, day after day, to make prints for the exhibition and book. Christophe Gielen and Sergio Purtell also made prints.

Walter Keller of Scalo courageously agreed to publish this book in its entirety. I'm grateful to him for understanding what I was up to, and to Hans Werner Holzwarth for his intelligent design.

Many friends helped edit this book. I would especially like to thank Susan Bell, Mitch Epstein, Louise Neri, and Iris Tillman Hill, who gave so generously of their time. As always, my husband Tom McDonough went over every word. In addition, Phil Bennett, Maurice Berger, Robert Coles, James Danziger, Chris Dercon, Alma Guillermoprieto, Katy Homans, Ben Lifson, Wendy MacNeil, Susan Meiselas, Jack Murrah, Nan Richardson, Fred Ritchin and Ellen Rudolph have supported and challenged me over the years. Without them none of this work would have been possible.

I know how to take pictures and I enjoy taking them in my leisure time.

I think about the pictures I'm going to take. I do. They must come out nicely. The person that I took mustn't say that I just took a picture that goes nowhere.

Other people want to see my camera — take it and look at it. It's their first time. I feel happy because people are looking at me like I'm a star. I am.

Pictures are worthwhile to remember something. It's the most important thing about them—to remember something about the past, but not the horrible past, the nice past, nice things you had once.

I keep my pictures in an album in my mother's drawer. I look at them sometimes when there's nothing I'm doing. I try to remember how it was when I took the picture. I think of the pictures rewinding and going back like a cassette — all those things happening over again.

I imagine looking at the pictures two years from now. I'll think about how it was when I was still small and how I was taking the pictures. If I become a photographer, I'll think how great I did.

— Palesa Molahloe, Soweto 1992

Wendy Ewald — Secret Games

Editing: Alexis Schwarzenbach
Design: Hans Werner Holzwarth, Berlin
Scans: Gert Schwab / Steidl, Schwab Scantechnik, Göttingen
Printing: Steidl, Göttingen
© 2000 for photographs and texts: Wendy Ewald
© 2000 for the photographs by Kentucky children: Appalshop
© 2000 for this edition: Scalo Zurich – Berlin – New York
Head office: Weinbergstrasse 22a, CH-8001 Zurich / Switzerland,
phone 41 1 261 0910, fax 41 1 261 9262,
e-mail publishers@scalo.com, website www.scalo.com
Distributed in North America by D.A.P., New York City;
in Europe, Africa and Asia by Thames and Hudson, London;
in Germany, Austria and Switzerland by Scalo.

All rights reserved. No part of this book may be
reproduced without the written permission of the publishers
or the artist.

First Scalo Edition 2000
ISBN 3-908247-28-4
Printed in Germany